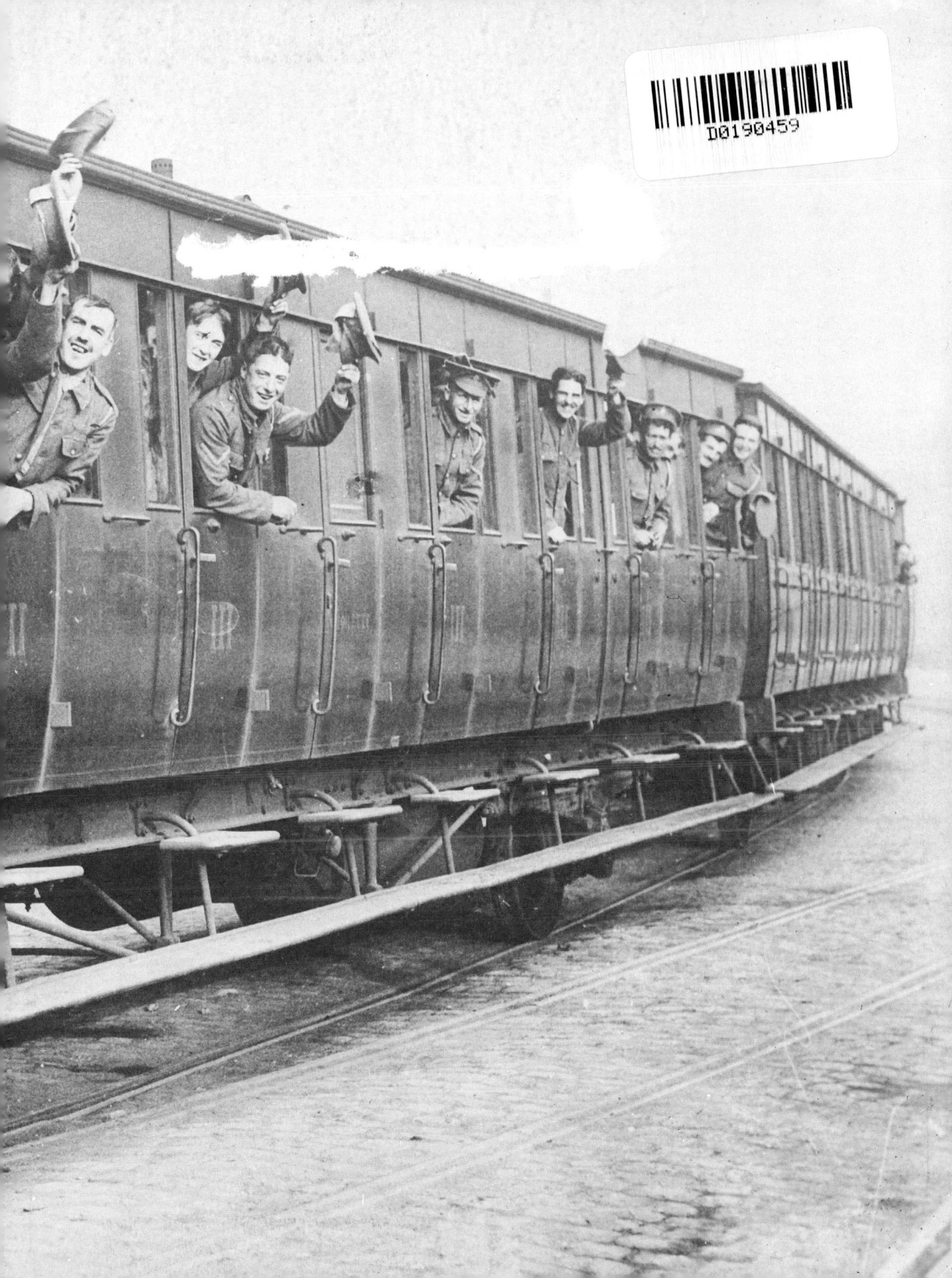

RAILWAYS
OF
THE GREAT WAR
WITH
MICHAEL PORTILLO

www.transworldbooks.co.uk

COLETTE HOOPER

RAILWAYS
— OF —
THE GREAT WAR
— WITH —
MICHAEL PORTILLO

BANTAM PRESS

LONDON · TORONTO · SYDNEY · AUCKLAND · JOHANNESBURG

TRANSWORLD PUBLISHERS
61–63 Uxbridge Road, London W5 5SA
A Random House Group Company
www.transworldbooks.co.uk

First published in Great Britain
in 2014 by Bantam Press
an imprint of Transworld Publishers

A CIP catalogue record for this book
is available from the British Library.

ISBN 9780593074121

Addresses for Random House Group Ltd companies outside the UK
can be found at: www.randomhouse.co.uk
The Random House Group Ltd Reg. No. 954009

The Random House Group Limited supports the Forest Stewardship Council® (FSC®),
the leading international forest-certification organisation. Our books carrying the
FSC label are printed on FSC®-certified paper. FSC is the only forest-certification
scheme supported by the leading environmental organisations, including Greenpeace.
Our paper procurement policy can be found at www.randomhouse.co.uk/environment

Typeset in Linoletter Std
Designed by Bobby Birchall, Bobby&Co
Printed in Germany

2 4 6 8 10 9 7 5 3 1

For Emmeline, my railway baby.

CONTENTS

ACKNOWLEDGEMENTS

I have advanced gingerly into this historical territory, where so many far more expert than I have trodden before me. Of the huge literature devoted to the First World War and to the railways, titles I have turned to again and again include David Stevenson's masterly overview of the conflict, *1914–1918: The History of the First World War*, and Christian Wolmar's accessible and inspiring railway histories, especially *Engines of War* and *Fire and Steam*. The two volumes of Edwin Pratt's *British Railways in the Great War*, published in 1921, are not for the faint-hearted but are a mine of detailed information unmatched elsewhere.

I must thank all the contributors interviewed for the series, too many to name but without whom neither the television programmes nor this book would be possible. I'm especially grateful to those who have given up their time to answer my questions and double-check facts. Special thanks are due to David Stevenson, who has acted as historical consultant to the programme and kindly reviewed this text. Of course, responsibility for any errors that remain is mine alone.

Colleagues past and present at Boundless have helped me build up my understanding of and passion for railway history over the last four years. I would particularly like to thank John Comerford for thinking of me for this project and Alison Kreps for her steady hand on the tiller; Tom Richardson and Bella Lloyd for sharing their research and contacts; and Rosie Wilcox and Giorgia Papapietro for their hard work on sourcing the images for this book. Chris Baker, thank you for your patience while I multitasked on this project and the programme.

Thanks to Cat Ledger for her encouragement throughout and to Michelle Signore for her clear vision. To Bobby Birchall for his beautiful design and especially to Ailsa Bathgate for her invaluable suggestions, clear corrections and moral support.

Special thanks to Michael Portillo, for writing the foreword but more importantly for his tireless commitment to sharing our rich railway history, come rain or shine, and to the BBC's Pam Cavannagh for steering us through this new railway venture.

A million thanks to Jane and Margaret – I couldn't have written this book without your backup.

Finally, thank you, Ian, for always believing in me, for all the late nights reading drafts and for inspiring me to make this book the best it could be.

PAGE 2 A Royal Engineers working party on the railway near Ypres on the Western Front in Belgium.

PAGE 6 Soldiers waving goodbye to loved ones as they leave Victoria Station in January 1915.

LEFT Female ticket collectors in 1915, filling the shoes of railwaymen sent to the Front.

FOREWORD BY MICHAEL PORTILLO

The railways helped to precipitate the First World War. They were the catalyst for mechanized war, enabling slaughter and destruction to occur on an unprecedented scale. Logistical skill or incompetence – organizing well or badly the trains that carried men, animals, food and shells – helped to determine the outcome of battles, arguably of the war. Eventually, an armistice was signed, in a railway carriage.

Because I had made numerous programmes about Britain's railways in the mid nineteenth century, I was used to thinking about the good that they had brought: for example, the increase in wealth through industrialization, fresh milk and fish to our cities, and seaside holidays for the working classes. In making these programmes about the First World War, I had to accept that its horrors could not have occurred without trains. No other transport system could have provided such an efficient conveyor belt, carrying millions of men to the trenches and tons of high explosive to annihilate them.

Accepting that that was the role allotted to railways, I began to delve into the human efforts involved in adapting them to total war. In Britain, the rail companies were huge employers, and their workers were skilled with machinery. They worked with pride and a highly developed sense of common purpose. Lord Kitchener's call for army volunteers attracted vast numbers of railwaymen.

The names of many appear on memorials at our railway stations. It is worth pausing by them, now that the centenary of their deaths is upon us. Men plucked from the footplate, signal boxes and ticket offices died on the Somme or in a hundred other battles.

Britain's mobilization was deftly managed. Sixty-eight thousand soldiers of the British Expeditionary Force were conveyed by train mainly to Southampton by the end of August 1914, and thence to the Continent. They arrived in time to fight at Mons and to make a difference. Might German forces have reached Paris in their absence? The railway companies also produced their ambulance trains by the end of August, although nobody had foreseen that they would have to be taken to France, where they handled unbelievable numbers of casualties.

Despite the efficiency of the British mobilization, in the following year we faced a chronic shortage of shells. Eric Geddes, a railway manager

RIGHT Michael Portillo on location at Fort Nelson, near Portsmouth.

through and through, was detached from the North Eastern Railway to deal with the crisis, and then to build and organize railways at the Front. He is a contender for the title 'The man who won the war', but he could rely on a large number of troops drawn from the railways, men who laid and re-laid tracks, cleared wreckage and kept locomotives running, under the screams of artillery.

The British Army understood the need to keep its millions of soldiers – and their horses – fed. Reliable supplies of rations, sufficiently high in calories for men working and fighting in trenches, were dispatched by train and conveyed to the dugouts. In the final stages of the war, as German soldiers went hungry, the British advantage may have been decisive.

At home, the appearance of Britain was changed. Young women greatly outnumbered young men. Many children had a father away on service or dead. The factories and railways were short of men, and women had to be recruited. Pre-war suffragettes helped to recruit 'munitionettes', who filled the artillery shells with explosives. Women (some in breeches) appeared in signal boxes, as porters and even station mistresses.

The First World War was a railway war like no other. It was different from previous European conflicts, because by 1914 the railways had reached such a high degree of development that all war planning on the Continent depended on efficient mobilization by rail – in a process that, once launched, was evidently unstoppable. A generation later, at the time of the Second World War, the lorry, jeep and tank were advanced enough to reduce somewhat armies' reliance on trains.

A century on from the outbreak of the First World War, historians and the public are trying to understand its causes and its course better. I for one had never realized until now that it *was* a railway war. Grasping that helps us to appreciate how commanders planned offensives and defined objectives. The general who did not grasp logistics was headed for defeat. Britain was moving in that direction until it tackled the shell crisis of 1915 and the bottlenecks on the railways in France and Belgium the following year.

Nearly a hundred years after the world's first locomotives had run in Britain, the advances in technology and industry, spurred on by railways, had created weapons with awful destructive power that humankind apparently could not control. Humanity had never previously had to wrestle with that thought, but it's remained a haunting issue for us ever since.

Making this television series about the railways in the First World War has been a more sombre task than following leads in a *Bradshaw's* handbook, as I have done previously. There's an inescapable poignancy in visiting the sites of battles on the Western Front, or even the faint traces of where munitions factories once stood. But my guess is that there is presently a national mood to remember, and to honour, those who toiled at home and fought abroad.

After the war's end, a railway wagon brought back to Britain the remains of an unknown soldier. For nearly a hundred years we have paid tribute at his tomb, honouring through him approximately a million British Empire troops who died and millions more from the other belligerent powers.

If the unknown soldier can be a symbol for slaughter on an incomprehensible scale, then perhaps those names on railway station memorials can also be a proxy, enabling us to salute all those who served and suffered during that terrible conflict.

May 2014

INTRODUCTION BY COLETTE HOOPER

1914 – A RAILWAY WORLD

By the eve of the First World War, almost a century had passed since the birth of the railways in Britain. Forged in the crucible of the industrial revolution, they had carried its transformative effects throughout the country and beyond – the embodiment of and the engine for extraordinary economic growth. By 1900, almost half a million miles of tracks had been laid across the globe. And as shining steam locomotives flew along the rails, billowing clouds of smoke and steam, the modern world grew up in their wake. Britain had led the way as industrialization, urbanization and mechanization took hold across Europe. By the turn of the twentieth century, the Railway Age appeared to be an era of unstoppable progress.

This period of rapid industrial expansion was also one of unprecedented peace on the Continent. Since 1815 there had been no

BELOW *Locomotion No. 1* – George Stephenson's engine, built for the Stockton and Darlington railway, the world's first public railway, opened in 1825.

war involving all the Great Powers. By the early twentieth century, some people believed that there never would be again. In June 1913, *The Economist* referred to trends 'which are slowly but surely making war between the civilised communities of the world an impossibility'. Two months later, a magnificent 'Peace Palace', intended as the home of international arbitration and funded by Andrew Carnegie – whose entrepreneurial career had begun on the railways – was opened at The Hague.

This forward-looking world ran to the rhythm of the railway. Just as today the internet seems omnipresent, so, on the eve of the First World War, the railways were woven into the fabric of everyday life. In Edwardian Britain, commuters set out from recently built suburbs each morning. Cheap trains carried industrial workers to and from their jobs in smoky manufacturing towns, and summer specials whisked them off to fresher climes for their annual holidays. Indeed, all along Britain's coasts, flourishing seaside resorts from Blackpool to Brighton benefited from the arrival of the railways, which had also opened up the wild beauty of some of Britain's remotest corners to new waves of tourists.

By now, people had grown used to the sight of the tracks that cut a swathe through the countryside. To the Victorians, who had witnessed their extraordinarily rapid multiplication, they had been a blot on the landscape. But vast viaducts that loomed over valleys and tunnels that plunged into hillsides had since become part of the scenery. In the cities, railway stations were key landmarks, while beneath Britain's capital the labyrinth of tunnels that housed the pioneering Underground continued to grow.

Londoners, along with all the other teeming urban populations that characterized industrial Britain, relied on the railways to feed them, and as well as staples the railways carried to the inner cities fresh delicacies, from Hampshire watercress to Yorkshire rhubarb. In the opposite

direction, news and information radiated out along the railway lines. Trains carried newspapers and letters, while the telegraph wires that followed the tracks – initially used in Britain by railway operators for signalling – provided ordinary people with the means to send messages over vast distances at unmatched speed.

As the railways developed, they had become big business for Britain. Right from the start, entrepreneurs realized there was money to be made from this new technology, and in the 1840s Britain had witnessed an extraordinary railway-building bubble. At the peak of this so-called 'railway mania', between 1844 and 1847, a staggering 9,500 miles of lines – the equivalent of 90 per cent of today's railway network – were authorized by Parliament. Amazingly, despite the inevitable crash that followed the boom, two-thirds of these lines went on to be built. During this Victorian free-market free-for-all, new railway companies proliferated throughout the land, and on the eve of the First World War Britain boasted a multitude of mostly thriving railway concerns.

At the top of the pile were the big players – the most powerful of which were the London and North Western, the Great Western, the Midland and the North Eastern. These companies oversaw huge railway empires that were about far more than simply running trains. They managed huge engineering works – indeed, in places like Swindon whole new towns had grown up to serve their operations. They owned horses, motor vehicles and steamships; they even ran hotels. To showcase their power and wealth, they had poured money into ostentatious buildings, such as the remarkable station and hotel complex at St Pancras, built by the Midland Railway in the 1860s. But there were also plenty of middling enterprises and dozens of smaller railway operators, some responsible for just a few miles of track. Some 600,000 people depended on the railways for their livelihoods, among them some of Britain's top engineering talent and sharpest business minds.

BELOW Hampstead Underground station, which opened in 1907.

17

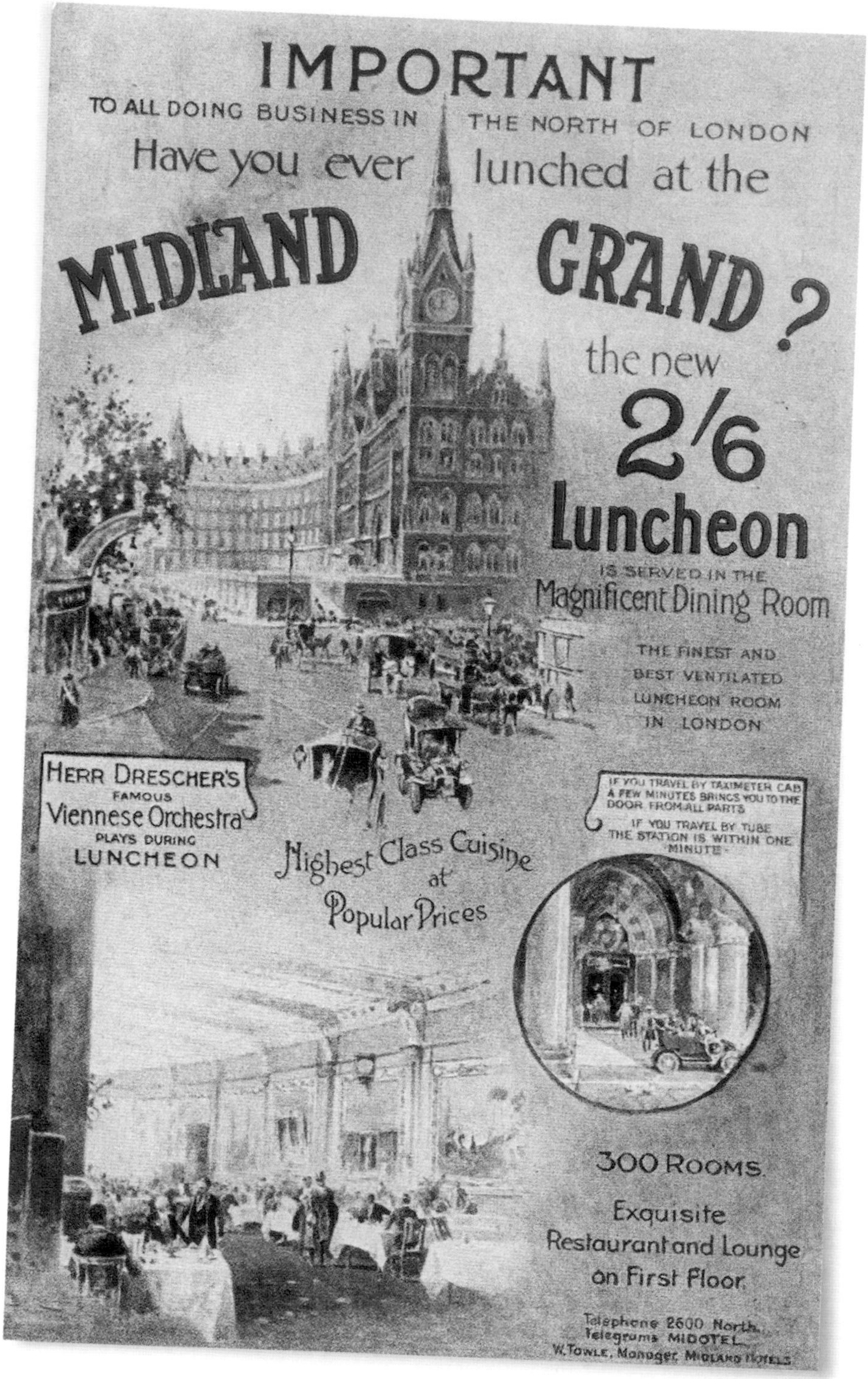
IMPORTANT
TO ALL DOING BUSINESS IN THE NORTH OF LONDON
Have you ever lunched at the
MIDLAND GRAND?
the new
2/6
Luncheon
IS SERVED IN THE
Magnificent Dining Room
THE FINEST AND
BEST VENTILATED
LUNCHEON ROOM
IN LONDON
HERR DRESCHER'S
FAMOUS
Viennese Orchestra
PLAYS DURING
LUNCHEON
IF YOU TRAVEL BY TAXIMETER CAB
A FEW MINUTES BRINGS YOU TO THE
DOOR FROM ALL PARTS
IF YOU TRAVEL BY TUBE
THE STATION IS WITHIN ONE
MINUTE
Highest Class Cuisine
at
Popular Prices
300 ROOMS.
Exquisite
Restaurant and Lounge
on First Floor.
Telephone 2600 North.
Telegrams MIDOTEL.
W. TOWLE, Manager, MIDLAND HOTELS

COPYRIGHT LON 89

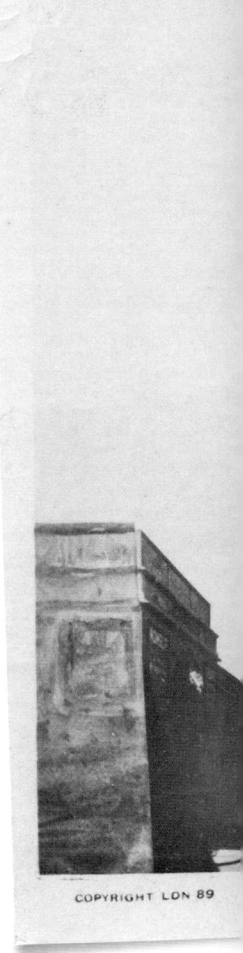

ST. PANCRAS STATION. LONDON.
(MIDLAND RAILWAY.)

LILYWHITE LTD.
ALL BRITISH PHOTO PRINTERS.

ABOVE AND LEFT The Midland Grand Hotel at St Pancras – a grandiose expression of the ambition and power of Britain's Victorian railway companies.

And of course countless other industries relied on the rails. From factories that had sprung up alongside the tracks in the nineteenth century, British industry exported its products across the globe. Steel from Port Talbot, lace from Nottingham, pen nibs from Birmingham and biscuits from Reading – the railways carried them all.

Many of the consumers for these products were denizens of the vast British Empire. The mother country had been quick to see the value of exporting locomotive technology to its Colonies and Dominions, and had overseen ambitious railway-building schemes in India, Canada and elsewhere. In conjunction with steamships, another nineteenth-century innovation, these tracks opened up new markets for British goods but also carried cheap imports, cutting prices for British consumers of all sorts of products from wheat to cocoa.

The railways were the arteries of this newly globalized economy, and the tracks were also a vital tool for exerting political power. Across the British Empire, they reinforced Britain's authority – a very visible reminder that troops could arrive swiftly to suppress dissent. By the early twentieth century, other European powers – notably Germany – were seeking to extend their own sphere of influence, and railways were an ideal means of doing so. Indeed, in the early years of the twentieth century, new railway routes such as the German-financed Berlin–Baghdad railway, which promised to give Germany a foothold in the Persian Gulf, became a source of international friction.

Within Europe, however, to most people it must have seemed as if railway expansion had brought nations closer. In 1870, there were some 64,000 miles of tracks in Europe. By 1914, that figure had almost tripled to 180,000 miles. This impressive network encouraged unprecedented numbers of travellers to board trains to explore the Continent. In the

1860s, the South Eastern and Chatham railway recorded an average of 310,000 people crossing the Channel each year. By 1913, more than 1.2 million were making the trip.

Never had the sights of Europe been within such easy reach. Well-heeled tourists from Britain could experience the Belle Epoque in all its glory. They could marvel at Art Nouveau Paris and catch the sun on the French Riviera before having a flutter in the Casino at Monte Carlo. Germany's Rhine attracted trainloads of tourists, who disembarked to enjoy paddle-steamer excursions, remarking on the castles that lined the river's banks – romantic relics of a violent past that was surely gone for ever. In Switzerland, extraordinary feats of railway engineering carried tourists to the very mountain peaks, where they could sample the new-found thrills of winter sports. And travellers bound for Constantinople could simply revel in the journey itself, on board a luxurious 'Orient Express'.

BELOW Early twentieth-century tourists flocked to Switzerland to marvel at the mountains from the comfort of the railway.

LEFT The Orient Express started running in the late nineteenth century and came to epitomize the glamour of international rail travel.

Right up to the eve of war, pleasure-seekers continued consulting railway timetables to plan their next adventure, oblivious to signs that the optimistic world of the Belle Epoque was slipping away. Behind its glittering facade, it was possible to glimpse portents of the trauma that lay ahead. Diplomatic crises periodically raised the spectre of war. And throughout the preceding century, while the Great Powers refrained from entering into a general conflict, the peace was punctured by smaller clashes, including the Crimean War of 1854–6 and the Franco-Prussian War of 1870–1. Even while builders at The Hague laboured to construct the Peace Palace, government spending on armaments grew ever more extravagant. In a *Times* article of September 1913 it was projected that: 'At the present rate of increase, Europe in ten years more would be spending on armaments annually a sum nearly sufficient to replace the mercantile marine of the whole world as it stands to-day.'

When the cataclysm came, it brought the express train of optimistic progress to a juddering halt. The outbreak of war sent tourists and expatriates racing to the railway stations, desperate to return to their home countries. In the interconnected world that the railways had helped to create, the violence quickly rippled outwards. The fruits of industrialization became the instruments of a mechanized war. And the railways, that emblem of civilization, were called to the service of a barbaric conflict, where cutting-edge technology would soon be juxtaposed with the primitive conditions of the trenches.

1914–1918 – THE RAILWAY WAR

The tracks and trains that had dominated European life in peacetime were destined also to dominate it in war. Railways were influencing military strategy before a shot was fired. They influenced where the war was fought and helped entrench the stalemate. Trains carried deadly weapons, ammunition, supplies and soldiers to the battlefields. And as total war extended its reach ever further, Britain's powerful rail industry was forced to make changes that ultimately altered the course of our railway history.

From the exploits of railwaymen at the Front to the secrets of railway spies who worked behind enemy lines; the manufacture of munitions

RIGHT Railway technology applied to war on the Western Front.

in railway workshops to the role of railways in post-war remembrance – this book explores some of the remarkable stories of the railway war. Individually, each illuminates a different aspect of the conflict. Taken together, they provide us with a fresh perspective on the First World War as a whole.

As we dig deeper into the war's railway history, new themes emerge and we see familiar stories from a different angle. Learning about the military planners' reliance on the railways helps us to understand why the conflict snowballed so quickly. By building up a picture of the vast quantities of materiel carried by the railways to the trenches, we better comprehend the extraordinary scale of the operations on the Western Front. Tracing the evolution of transport policy over the course of the war demonstrates how, even in the years of stalemate, tactics were constantly changing as both sides innovated to try to break the deadlock. And by discovering how railway managers helped political and military leaders learn how to wage industrial war, we revive the memory of forgotten figures who shaped the war's history.

On the home front, focusing on the railway story highlights the extent to which the war changed civilian lives, as British passengers jostled with military traffic on the lines and railwaymen were replaced by women workers on the tracks. Many of those railway employees who went to war never returned. By exploring how they were mourned, we can begin to understand the shock waves of grief that spread throughout the nation in the aftermath of the conflict.

RIGHT The railways carried millions of men and huge quantities of munitions to the front line.

In the hundred years that have passed since the outbreak of the First World War, countless books have been written about the causes and course of the conflict. It has become a much-contested area of historical debate. But what cannot be disputed is the fundamental role played by the railways and those who worked on them. As we try to pick a path through this turbulent period in our history, we can follow the tracks of the railway war – from the twilight of the Belle Epoque, through the carnage of the fighting and into the shell-shocked post-war world.

RIGHT In France and on the home front, the sights and sounds of steam locomotion were the backdrop to the war.

CHAPTER 1

A RAILWAY WAR BEGINS

EUROPE'S RAILWAY WAR PLANS ARE BORN

Long before the First World War had begun, it was destined to be a railway war. In the decades leading up to the eruption of violence, all the major players on the international stage readied themselves for conflict, and the thousands of miles of track criss-crossing the continent were at the heart of their plans.

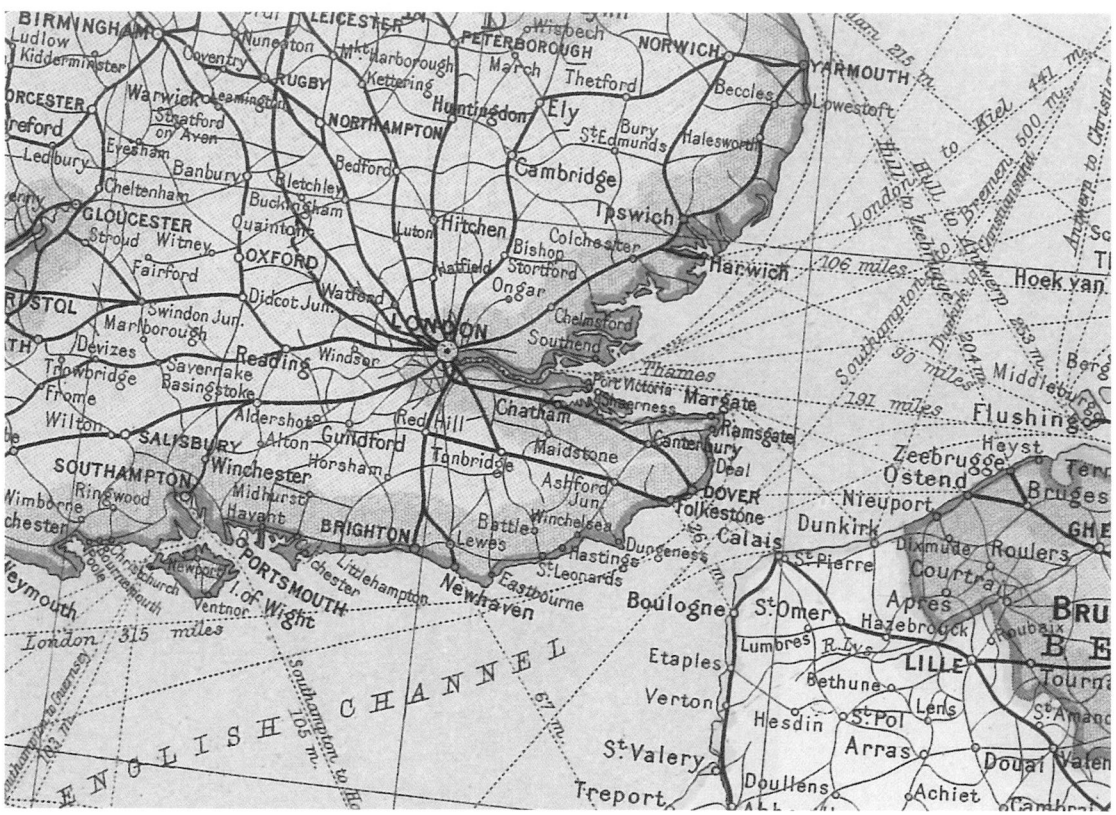

In the second half of the nineteenth century, as the rail network unfurled across the globe, military leaders began to wake up to its potential. Conflicts that flared up in this period provided a training ground for the use of railways in war. When France and the German state of Prussia came to blows in 1870, both sides discovered that using the power of locomotion to shift men and materiel could be decisive in determining the outcome of battle. During the Anglo-Boer War in South Africa in 1899–1902, Britain also experimented with railway strategy,

ABOVE AND OVERLEAF
A railway map of central Europe at the end of the nineteenth century.

using armoured trains for the first time. The Age of Steam had given birth to a new means of projecting military might.

While the armed forces were familiarizing themselves with rail power, deeper changes were afoot. Between 1870 and 1914, the railways helped usher in a second industrial revolution in Europe. The continent's advanced economies boomed, its population mushroomed from 293 million to 490 million and there was a surge of technological innovations, including the development of deadly new weapons of war.

By the early twentieth century, Britain had lost its position as the leading industrialized European economy to a newly unified Germany. And as the German Empire grew in strength, Europe's delicate balance of power looked increasingly fragile. New alliances were forged and consolidated, splitting the continent's strongest states into two opposing power blocs. Nations flexed their military muscle, developing policies of mass conscription and stockpiling armaments. The scent of war was in the air, and with vast, heavily armed forces to transport, railways would be vital. By 1914, the Great Powers all had plans in place to mobilize millions of men by rail, delivering them into battle at record speed.

Perhaps the ultimate expression of railway war planning was found in the German Empire. Indeed, the whole German military strategy depended on the railways. By the early twentieth century, Germany was surrounded by potential enemies. To the west was its old foe France; to the east, Russia, which in 1892 had turned its back on Germany in favour of an alliance with the French. Despite the formidable strength of the German imperial military, its leaders knew that any attempt to fight a two-front war would be doomed to defeat. But the railways seemed to offer a tantalizing way out of the trap.

The idea was daring. First dreamt up at the turn of the twentieth century by Chief of the Imperial German General Staff, Alfred von Schlieffen, it was based on the premise that Russia, with a sparse railway network and vast distances to cover, could not mobilize troops as quickly as Germany. Schlieffen thus proposed that in the event of war, the bulk of Germany's men could initially be deployed westwards to rapidly overwhelm France. They would then turn back in time to meet the Russians.

After Schlieffen's retirement, he was succeeded in 1906 by Helmuth von Moltke, who made some amendments to the strategy. But the essence of the so-called 'Schlieffen Plan' remained unchanged: troops would

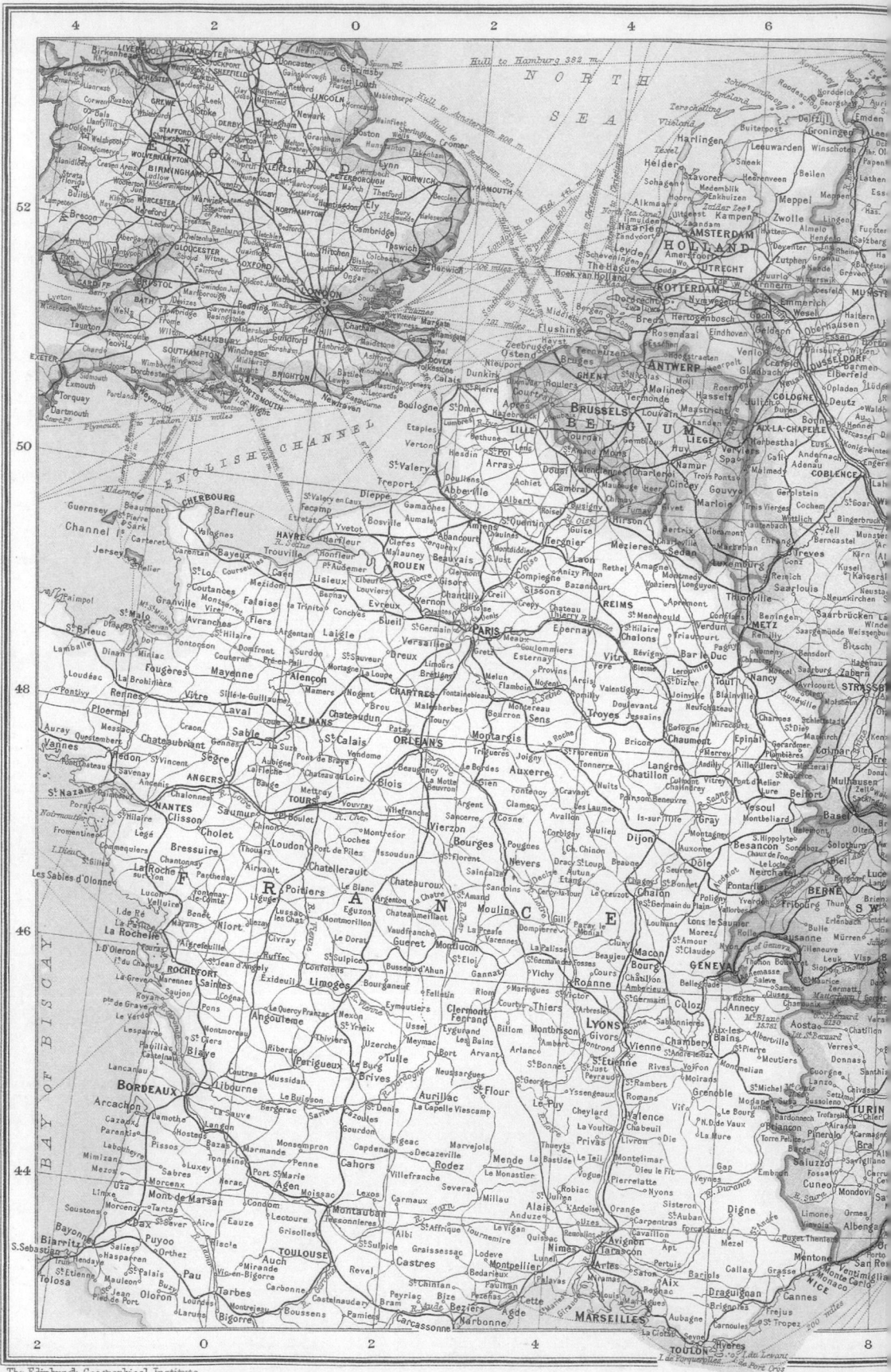

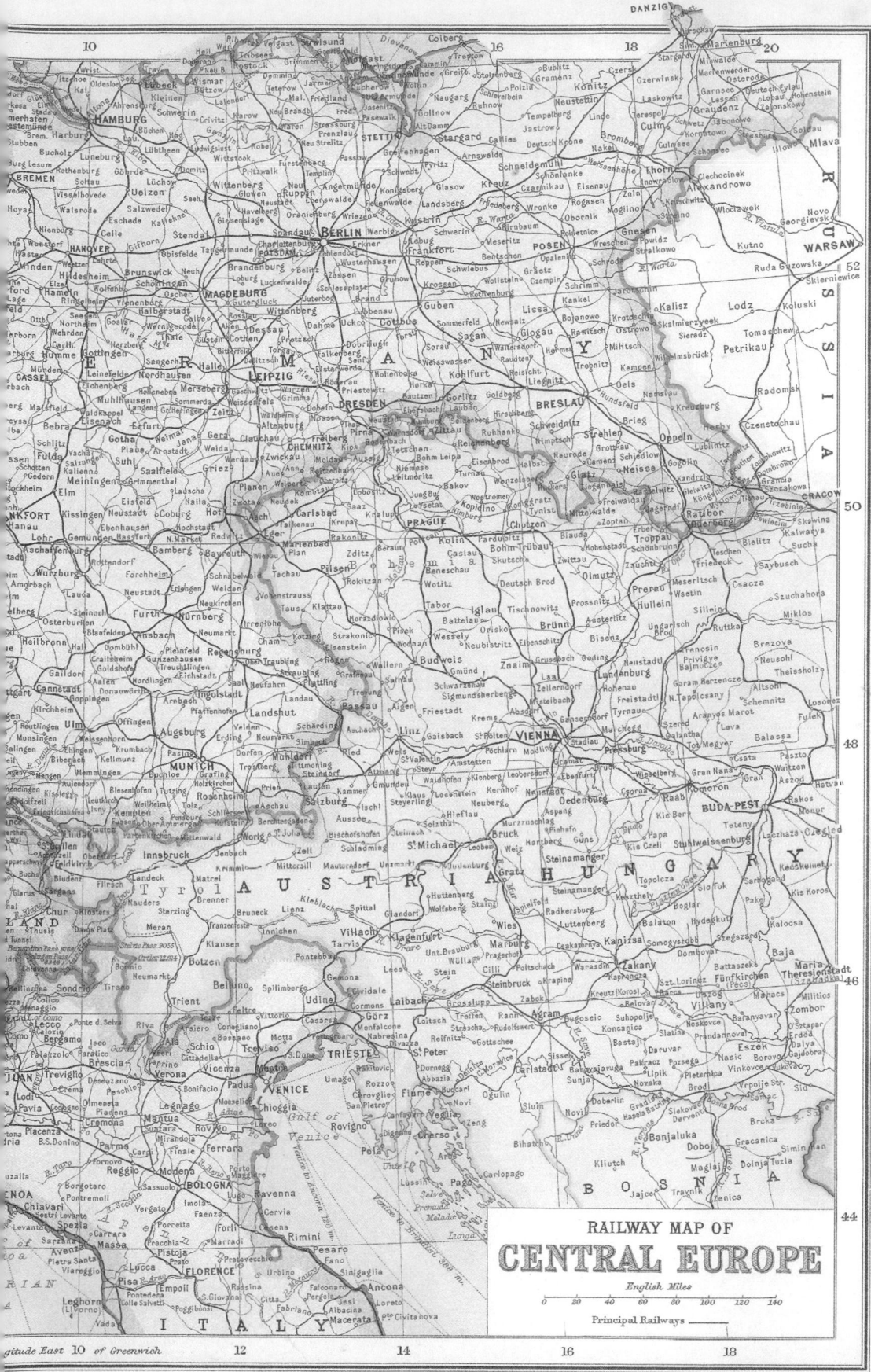

RAILWAY MAP OF
CENTRAL EUROPE

English Miles

0   20   40   60   80   100   120   140

Principal Railways ————

John Bartholomew & Co.

LEFT General Helmuth von Moltke the Younger, Schlieffen's successor as Chief of the German General Staff.

advance through the Low Countries, avoiding the fortresses that flanked the Franco-German frontier and taking advantage of the impressive Belgian railway network. They would then encircle Paris, crushing the French army, before rushing back to the Eastern Front by rail.

Extensive preparations were made for this railway advance. New lines were built towards Germany's western borders and existing ones were double-tracked to improve capacity. Key junctions were expanded, with new marshalling yards added. And all along the most important routes, platforms were extended to facilitate the loading and unloading of military trains. Still today, the legacy of this can be seen along the border, where seemingly insignificant towns have stations with incongruously long platforms.

Alongside this investment in infrastructure, the logistics were meticulously thought through and rehearsed. In the event of war, the German military would take immediate control of the railways. Revised annually, intricate timetables provided for the transport of millions of men to the frontiers. Every detail was considered, right down to the transport of carrier pigeons on troop trains.

Meanwhile, the French were also laying the groundwork for a railway war. Between 1870 and 1913, they quadrupled the number of lines to the German border from four to sixteen. As in Germany, France's military strategy rested on the mobilization of men by rail. By 1914, the French Chief of the General Staff was former military engineer and railway expert Joseph Joffre. His 'Plan XVII', the French equivalent to the Schlieffen-Moltke Plan, provided for a rapid response to a possible German invasion. The idea was to use the railways to launch an aggressive counter-attack, stopping the Germans in their tracks. The plan was flexible, allowing the commander to wait until the last minute to decide exactly where to strike.

But France wasn't just concerned with its own railways. France's security relied on its principal ally, Russia, being able to send its army speedily to the German frontier. Russia had vast numbers of men at its disposal, but its railways lagged behind those in western Europe. In order for Russia to pose a credible threat to Germany, this would have to change. Rail improvements topped the agenda at talks between France and Russia, and France made loans to its ally to finance the building of new lines.

Of course, railways cannot be built in secret, and as the pace of strategic tracks being laid increased in the pre-war years, the Great Powers eyed their rivals' projects uneasily. The railway 'arms race' served to ratchet up fear and mistrust between nations, providing leaders with justification for further bolstering their own war preparations. This tit-for-tat spiral all but guaranteed that war, when it came, would bring destruction on an unprecedented scale.

Intelligence about new lines was seized on by all sides, including Britain. By analysing patterns of railway building, some military observers guessed that Germany was getting ready for a potential invasion of France via Belgium. Although Britain had aligned itself with France and Russia, and vowed to protect Belgian neutrality, it was far from certain whether British forces would fight in a future Continental war. But contingency plans were quietly being made for that very eventuality.

BELOW French Chief of the General Staff Joseph Joffre, a former military engineer and railway expert.

With fighting unlikely to take place on British soil, railway planning took a rather different guise. In any case, new construction was far less important, as the birthplace of the railways already had an excellent network of tracks. Indeed, thanks to Victorian railway mania, many areas had surplus capacity. Nevertheless, timetables were drawn up to enable the efficient dispatch of a fighting force to the Continent. Britain also arranged for close coordination with its powerful railway companies in the event of war. From 1912, the top managers of the biggest of these corporations sat on a secret Railway Executive Committee, poised to take over the running of the national network should conflict break out.

The need for effective cooperation between the railway industry and the military in wartime was spelled out in guidance disseminated by British planners in the run-up to war. A pocket-sized publication entitled *Railway Manual (War)* was published by His Majesty's Stationery Office, the government publishers, in 1911. This booklet provided the military with all the information they needed to seize the levers of control of the railways in the event of war. It described the military chain of command on the tracks, from the Director of Railways at the top to individual Railway Control Officers on the ground. There were tips on planning the movement of supplies, including a handy guide for the amount of wagon space to allocate for a given tonnage of biscuits or munitions. It even contained sample copies of wartime paperwork, such as warrants for military travel to be issued in lieu of tickets.

But the overwhelming message of the *Railway Manual* was that running railways was too complicated for the armed forces to manage alone: 'So delicate and complex a matter is railway management that the efficient operation of a railway system can only be ensured when the cordial cooperation of railwaymen is combined with the strictest obedience of regulations by the troops.'

For railways to reach their military potential, the manual argued, soldiers had to bow to the expertise of the army of railway workers who knew the tricks of the trade. Should servicemen forget this and interfere in matters they did not understand – for example, by using locomotive water supplies for drinking water – chaos would surely follow.

Little did the authors realize just how intertwined the rail industry and the war effort were to become. But they did not have long to wait to find out. Just three years later, the book was being reprinted with important modifications, because Britain and its railways were at war.

RIGHT The British *Railway Manual (War)* – this volume contained the information required by the military to make efficient use of the railways in wartime.

RAILWAY MANUAL

(WAR).

120
Mobn.
72

LONDON:
PUBLISHED BY HIS MAJESTY'S STATIONERY OFFICE.
To be purchased, either directly or through any Bookseller, from
WYMAN AND SONS, LIMITED, FETTER LANE, E.C.; or
OLIVER AND BOYD, TWEEDDALE COURT, EDINBURGH; or
E. PONSONBY, LTD., 116, GRAFTON STREET, DUBLIN.

PRINTED BY
HARRISON AND SONS, PRINTERS IN ORDINARY TO HIS MAJESTY,
45-47, ST. MARTIN'S LANE, W.C.

1911.

Price Sixpence.

WAR BY TIMETABLE – THE CLIMAX TO THE RAILWAY AGE?

Ever since the end of the First World War, debate has raged over the causes of this cataclysmic event. Experts have looked for answers in the detailed records of diplomatic discussions; they've examined long-term economic trends; they've assessed the role of public patriotism. But for one of Britain's best-known historians, railway timetables held the key.

A. J. P. Taylor (1906–90) wrote some of the biggest-ever-selling works on the First World War, and his television broadcasts brought his interpretation of events to an even wider audience. For him, the conflict was the 'unexpected climax to the railway age'. He believed that no one really wanted war in 1914. Instead, it was 'imposed on the statesmen of Europe by railway timetables'.

LEFT The historian A. J. P. Taylor. In *War by Timetable*, he emphasized the influence of railway plans on the outbreak of the First World War.

Taylor argued that the railway plans made by all the Great Powers were originally intended as a deterrent. To intimidate their rivals, each nation built up vast armies of conscripts and designed elaborate plans to mobilize them by rail.

However, as the plans evolved, they developed fatal flaws that were to lead Europe inexorably towards war. First, they were based on the idea that speed was of the essence: 'Whichever power completed its mobilization first would strike first and might even win the war before the other side was ready.' Once one nation had begun to mobilize, its enemies were forced to follow or risk being left behind.

Second, while the majority of the Great Powers could commence mobilization without declaring war, aggression was built in to the German war plans. Implementing the Schlieffen-Moltke Plan meant invading Belgium within days of giving the order to mobilize. Once Germany's troop trains had started rolling, war was inevitable. And once begun, mobilization was impossible to stop: '... railway timetables cannot be improvised. Once started, the wagons and carriages must roll remorselessly and inevitably forward to their predestined goal. Horses can be stopped crossing a stream; railway carriages cannot.'

So, according to Taylor, as the international-relations crisis of July 1914 unfolded, the railway plans took on a life and unstoppable momentum of their own. 'Prisoners of their own weapons', Europe's leaders were powerless to halt the march to war.

In his brilliantly written books, A. J. P. Taylor made a compelling case. Today, however, the general consensus is that his analysis puts too much weight on the railway plans as an immediate catalyst of the war.

Taylor's views were informed by his politics. Writing at the height of the Cold War, he was critical of the idea of nuclear deterrence. His narrative of the First World War illustrated his beliefs about the potentially devastating unintended consequences of using the threat of mutual destruction to maintain the peace.

Historians who have followed him have shown that in fact the railway timetables were much more flexible than Taylor gave them credit for. Improvisation did take place on the tracks, for example in Britain where the mobilization timetables were rewritten right up to the last minute. Taylor's characterization of Europe's political and military elite as helpless and often foolish, blindly blundering towards catastrophe, has also been criticized. More recent interpretations suggest the leaders of the Great Powers made a conscious choice for war, aware of the consequences of their actions, if not of the way the conflict would eventually unfold.

However, while the detail of Taylor's argument has been contested, his vision of the First World War as 'the climax of the railway age' still stands. Railway-building programmes were part of a wider 'arms race' in the pre-war years, and as the number of lines serving border areas grew, they fuelled rising tension and mutual distrust between the rival nations.

And it is also true that the railway mobilization plans may have helped nudge the belligerent Great Powers closer to conflict. Every nation was convinced that attack was the best form of defence – delaying mobilization could therefore be catastrophic. Once one country's army was on the move, it was all too easy for mobilization to develop its own deadly momentum, as the events of the 'July Crisis' in 1914 were to prove. Once Russia had made the first move, mobilizing men 'just in case', Germany felt compelled to do likewise or risk being too late to avoid the dreaded two-front war. And with the violation of neutral countries fundamental to the German plan, events quickly snowballed into widespread war.

Without their railway plans, the Great Powers could never have sent millions of conscripts into action as they did. The beginning of the Great War would have looked very different. And whatever their role in its outbreak, the railways were to continue to shape the conflict for the next four years.

A FALSE START TO THE RAILWAY WAR – GERMANY INVADES A RAILWAY STATION IN LUXEMBOURG

Europe's railway plans were in place, and they were about to be tested. On 28 June 1914, Archduke Franz Ferdinand, heir to the Austro-Hungarian throne, was assassinated in Sarajevo in the name of South Slav nationalism. Simmering tensions between Austria-Hungary and its Serbian neighbour reached boiling point. And as the diplomatic rhetoric hotted up, global conflict seemed increasingly likely.

During the month of July, Europe's leaders tested one another's commitment to a complex system of alignments. Russia was inclined to protect Serbia, while Germany promised to back Austria-Hungary in the event of a Russian attack. As the two mighty nations readied themselves to enter the fray, there were fears of an unstoppable chain reaction, with France and perhaps also Britain coming to the aid of Russia, the third member of the Triple Entente.

On 28 July came the first declaration of war: diplomacy between Austria-Hungary and Serbia had broken down. In the words of Emperor Franz Joseph: 'The intrigues of a malevolent opponent compel me, in the defence of the honor of my Monarchy, for the protection of its dignity and its position as a power, for the security of its possessions, to grasp the sword after long years of peace.' Russia responded to this declaration by tentatively mobilizing men, demonstrating its readiness to support Serbia. Germany stood by, poised to pull the trigger on its own railway plans.

Finally, as July tipped into August, talk was irreversibly transformed into action. Tsar Nicholas II refused to demobilize. If Germany was to go ahead with the Schlieffen-Moltke Plan, it was now or never. By their calculations, the Russians would be at the border within a few short weeks. The pre-emptive attack on France had to be launched immediately. On 1 August, Germany declared war on Russia. And that very evening German troops made their first incursion onto foreign soil.

Unsurprisingly, this first act of German aggression involved the railways. More remarkable is where the war's opening move took place. We tend to think that the conflict began with the invasion of Belgium. But, in fact, hostilities commenced with the occupation of a small provincial station in the tiny Grand Duchy of Luxembourg. This forgotten railway story illuminates the often-overlooked role that Luxembourg played in the war and reveals how even the best-laid railway plans were not infallible.

Bordered on three sides by Germany, Belgium and France, Luxembourg's strategic importance had long been evident. It was pledged to neutrality in the event of a European conflict; however, the Grand Duchy of Luxembourg played a key role in the German war plans thanks to its status as an international rail hub.

The railway had arrived in Luxembourg in 1859 with a line that connected Luxembourg City with Thionville, then in France but annexed by Germany after the Franco-Prussian war. This exciting new technology was welcomed with open arms. A song penned in Luxembourgish to celebrate the coming of the rails became so popular that it was, for a time, a rival national anthem. Even today, Luxembourg's national motto is the last line of the chorus, which roughly translates as:

Come here from France, Belgium, Prussia,
We want to show you our fatherland
Ask in all directions,
We want to remain what we are.

By the turn of the twentieth century, this tiny state boasted an impressive network of tracks. Lines spread out from the capital to Belgium in the north, France to the south and west, and Germany in the east. Germany's military planners were well aware of the advantages control of this system could bring, and they envisaged that two east–west routes would provide vital direct supply lines for their troops in France as they swept to encircle Paris.

RIGHT The railway station at Troisvierges – the surprising site of the first German incursion into Luxembourg.

Luxembourg's rail network offered one further advantage. Right from the start, the country's railways were the product of international cooperation, with French loans used to fund the infrastructure, and services operated by the Compagnie des chemins de fer de l'Est. However, this situation changed after the Franco-Prussian War of 1870–1. The peace treaty stated that Luxembourg's railways, as well as those in the conquered territory of neighbouring Alsace-Lorraine, should come under the control of the victorious German Reich.

As part of the agreement, Germany promised never to use the railways for military purposes or in any way 'incompatible with the neutrality of the Grand Duchy'. But that promise was to be dramatically broken in 1914 when, on the evening of 1 August, a group of sixteen or so armed German soldiers drove up to the station at Troisvierges, an unassuming village near a major junction on the line north towards Belgium.

What happened next shocked the locals and the nation, and has left a puzzling record. A newspaper account in *L'Indépendance Luxembourgeoise* on 2 August 1914, uncovered and translated by local historian David Heal, recounts the story:

> *The Germans arrived in Troisvierges by vehicle and entered the Telegraph Office, revolvers in hand.*
>
> *An argument started between them and the Station Master. As the Germans wanted to confiscate the telegraph apparatus, the Station Master broke it and threw it on the floor.*
>
> *The Germans then went out. And for a distance of 150 metres in the direction of the Belgian frontier they unbolted the rails. Someone*

said to them, 'But you are on neutral territory'. 'We know', replied the officer. 'Shut up if you don't want us to sort you out'.

20 minutes later a military vehicle arrived. It carried orders for the first soldiers to leave, with a declaration according to which the first orders had been misunderstood.

With that, the invading force beat a hasty retreat back over the border, and it seems the whole bizarre incident lasted less than an hour. What lay behind this 'false start' to the fighting?

It seems that Germany's declaration of war against Russia gave the green light for the Schlieffen-Moltke Plan to begin cranking into action. The seizure of Troisvierges was to be one of the first steps. But meanwhile, unbeknownst to the boots on the ground, wrangling at the highest levels was threatening to disrupt their plans. Communications between Germany and Britain had given Germany the impression that the British might yet be persuaded to stay out of the conflict, and perhaps keep France out too. The German Emperor Kaiser Wilhelm II was keen to hold out for a clear answer before committing his troops. The order was

LEFT Kaiser Wilhelm II
of Germany.

sent out to delay the invasion of Luxembourg, but it was too late for the advance guard, who had already secured their objective, only to face the embarrassment of being recalled half an hour later.

It seems that even at the apogee of the railway age, with all the advantages of the telegraph and the telephone available, a simple breakdown in communication could lead to a major blunder – an accidental invasion. What remains more of a mystery is the actions of the troops. David Heal has analysed contemporary accounts and found they all agree that the soldiers tore up the tracks near Troisvierges station, but this would seem to directly contradict the invaders' aims. Why destroy the very lines that they were occupying the country to exploit? Perhaps it was a case of misunderstood orders, the first instance of many whereby carefully conceived plans turned out to be rather messier in the execution.

Whatever the truth, the 'real' invasion of Luxembourg was not delayed for long. Britain soon made clear to Germany that it would not remain neutral in the face of an attack on its French and Belgian allies, and the very next day armoured trains carried German soldiers across the border and right into the heart of Luxembourg city. This time, there was no mistaking the purpose of their presence. As a German army proclamation announced: 'The occupation of Luxembourg . . . has only one objective, to open the railway for future operations.' Despite repeated reminders from the government about the country's neutral status, no one stepped in to enforce it, and the locals were left reeling. An article in *L'Indépendance Luxembourgeoise* on 3 August vividly evokes the public mood:

> *When Luxembourg woke up on Sunday, the city was full of German uniforms. All day, on foot, on horseback, on bicycles, in vehicles, on motorcycles, German officers and soldiers never stopped moving.*

At the street corners, you will see, since then, the glint of bayonets.

In the lower town, a guard unit has been installed. Outside, there is not a road, not a footpath, which is not guarded. The railways are occupied by the military, the stations guarded. It is the German military which allows the trains to depart. All the Post Offices, with the exception of that in the city, are occupied by the German army.

The population of Luxembourg has been struck dumb by this occupation. You will find a few, a very few, who take it as a joke, but every other face, without exception, is astonished.

Luxembourg was to remain occupied until the end of the conflict. As well as maintaining control of the railways, the occupying forces imposed strict border controls and cracked down heavily on imports and exports. Luxembourgers suffered serious food shortages as a result, and soup kitchens were set up to help those most in need.

In many ways, Luxembourg's was the forgotten occupation of the First World War. The events of 1 and 2 August were soon eclipsed by the next step in the Schlieffen-Moltke Plan: mass mobilization for the long-planned advance on Paris, as the first of 11,000 trains carrying 3 million men rolled towards the Belgian border.

BELOW German soldiers occupying the station at Troisvierges during the war.

Partie vom Bahnhof ULFLINGEN mit Wagenburg der Landsturm Kompagnie

RAILWAY SABOTAGE – DERAILING
THE SCHLIEFFEN PLAN

The German plan for invading Belgium was staggeringly bold. First, troops were to capture the vital railway junction of Liège, near the German border. Then, approximately half a million men of the First and Second Armies would funnel through the junction, fanning out across the centre of the country to commence their grand sweep through to France. Simultaneously, the Third, Fourth and Fifth Armies would begin following their pre-planned routes, which passed through Belgium's southern provinces. Trains would disgorge troops at the border, from where the advancing masses would travel on horse and by foot. Behind them, the captured railway network would play an essential role, bringing in vital reinforcements and supplies.

The plans showed utter disregard for Belgian neutrality. But Belgium was not going to submit without a fight. To try to stop the Germans in

ABOVE A German wagon park at Troisvierges station.

their tracks, the Belgians were prepared to go to extreme lengths – even if that meant wrecking the infrastructure they had built up over a century.

Belgium in 1914 was a small country with an economy that punched above its weight, powered by an impressive rail network. The first Belgian line was built in 1835, making it the first European country after Britain to embrace train travel, and according to the 1913 edition of *Bradshaw's Continental Railway Guide*, by then more than 4,700 miles of tracks had been laid. Providing excellent connections to the rest of Europe, the railways helped Belgian industry to boom, and the area around Liège was the beating heart of this industrial powerhouse. The city is described in *Bradshaw's* as 'the centre of one of the most industrious districts of the country, with coal mines in the immediate vicinity, and iron foundries, engineering shops, and manufactories on all sides'. As such it was particularly well served by the railways, with double-tracked lines running east into Germany and west towards Brussels and Paris.

But while Belgium was an increasingly self-confident player in the

BELOW The Schlieffen-Moltke Plan, showing the intended routes for the German advance.

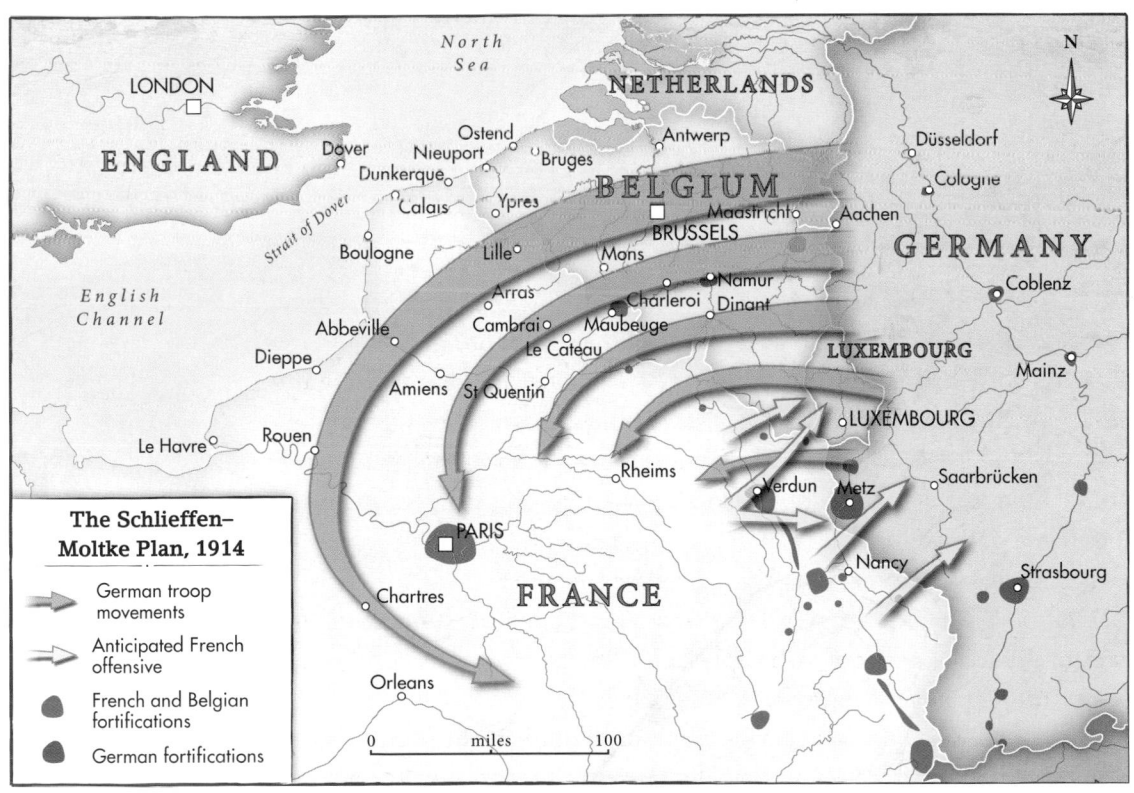

global economy, politically it was still finding its feet. The state of Belgium had only been officially created in 1831, after winning independence from the Netherlands. Aware of its weakness, since 1839 Belgium had promised to remain neutral in the event of war, backed by guarantees from all the main powers. However, as the century wore on it became clear that Belgian neutrality could easily be threatened. Perched uneasily between France and Germany, a route through Belgium might prove too tempting should either side wish to attack the other. The enviable rail system would surely only increase the allure to a would-be invader – the nation's pride and joy could well become its Achilles heel.

As early as the Franco-Prussian War in 1870, the Belgian authorities began to consider how to prevent their railways being exploited by an invading army. The proposed solution was radical: to destroy the very lines that gave them access to the country. And as the war clouds gathered in the early 1900s, secret plans were made for railway sabotage on a grand scale. Liège historian Christophe Bechet has uncovered memoranda produced by the First Directorate of Military Operations, part of the Belgian Ministry of War, which describe how this destructive mission was to take place.

The first line of defence was to be the pre-emptive demolition of important tunnels in the border area, to try to prevent an invasion before it had even begun. In the years running up to the outbreak of war, special mine cavities were built into the brickwork of tunnels. According to the plans, on the order of the King and the Minister of War, teams would be dispatched by rail to load them with explosives and await a telegram or telephone call giving the green light to detonate the charge.

Should this not suffice to deter the invaders, Belgian troops would then move to a plan of targeted demolitions. Paying close attention to the movements of the invading force, they would destroy or block strategic bridges, tunnels and embankments, trying to slow the pace of the advance. Civil employees of the railways also had a role to play, with directions to sabotage points, derail wagons, cut power lines and empty water tanks for locomotives – in short, to wreak maximum havoc on the rails.

This preparation for destruction was not in vain. On 2 August 1914, Belgium's worst fears were realized. Germany issued an ultimatum demanding free passage through Belgium and explicitly asking for the freedom of the railways. King Albert I refused point-blank. On 3 August, he gave the order to blow up tunnels on the key lines serving the border,

ABOVE An early postcard of Liège-Guillemins station.

LIÈGE   Gare des Guillemins

and, less than twenty-four hours later, the Germans began their assault on Belgium.

Christophe Bechet's research has revealed that the planned pre-emptive strike met with mixed success. In Luxembourg province, to the south-west of Liège, the planned sabotage went like clockwork, putting the railway lines out of action until the end of the month. However, in the crucial Liège area, things went badly wrong. Catastrophically, many of the carefully laid charges failed to detonate. Of the four tunnels scheduled for demolition, just one was successfully destroyed. Inexperience on the part of the Belgian soldiers and dud explosives stored in damp cellars were to blame. As an expedient, locomotives were derailed inside the tunnels, one on top of another. But the failure of the original plan enabled the Germans to carry out speedy repairs, establishing useful supply lines with relative ease.

The troops also made one further fatal error. Blocking the path of the German invasion was the natural barrier of the river Meuse, crossed in places by railway viaducts. In Namur province, Belgian and French troops successfully destroyed all these crossings. But the Belgian engineers of the Third Division, defending Liège, forgot to demolish the crucial Val-Benoit viaduct. The supplies of the First and Second German Armies were thus able to be transported across the river Meuse immediately after the capture of the city on 16 August.

Even where demolitions succeeded, German Eisenbahntruppen (railway troops) were prepared for sabotage and worked tirelessly to repair the damage, with impressive results. When it looked like it would take months to re-open the wrecked bridge near the town of Trois-Ponts, south-east of Liège, they built a whole new track and a bridge to bypass the problem. With the help of the forced labour of the local population, this was completed in less than four weeks.

Yet even as Belgium was being overrun, the sabotage effort continued. On Liège province's Stavelot–Pepinster line, railway employees hid signals and railway points, and even buried sections of the railway, at considerable risk to themselves. It took the invaders a fortnight to clear the line, and the railway employees suffered serious consequences, undergoing interrogation in their homes as German soldiers strove to uncover their hiding places.

Back in Britain, the popular press was helping to whip up widespread public sympathy for Belgium. The pages of the newspapers were filled with shocking tales of German atrocities against helpless civilians. Plucky Belgian railway saboteurs made for an irresistible story. Under the headline 'A Daring Feat', a 30 September 1914 issue of the *Taunton Courier* breathlessly recounts the destruction of a viaduct by a party of Belgian cyclists, before going on to describe an even more sensational act of sabotage:

LEFT King Albert of Belgium, who led the Belgian army during the First World War.

TOP RIGHT Inspection by German troops of the destroyed railway tunnel in Homburg, Belgium.

RIGHT One of the bridges over the river Meuse successfully destroyed by retreating Belgian troops.

Zerstörter Tunnel in Homburg, Belgien

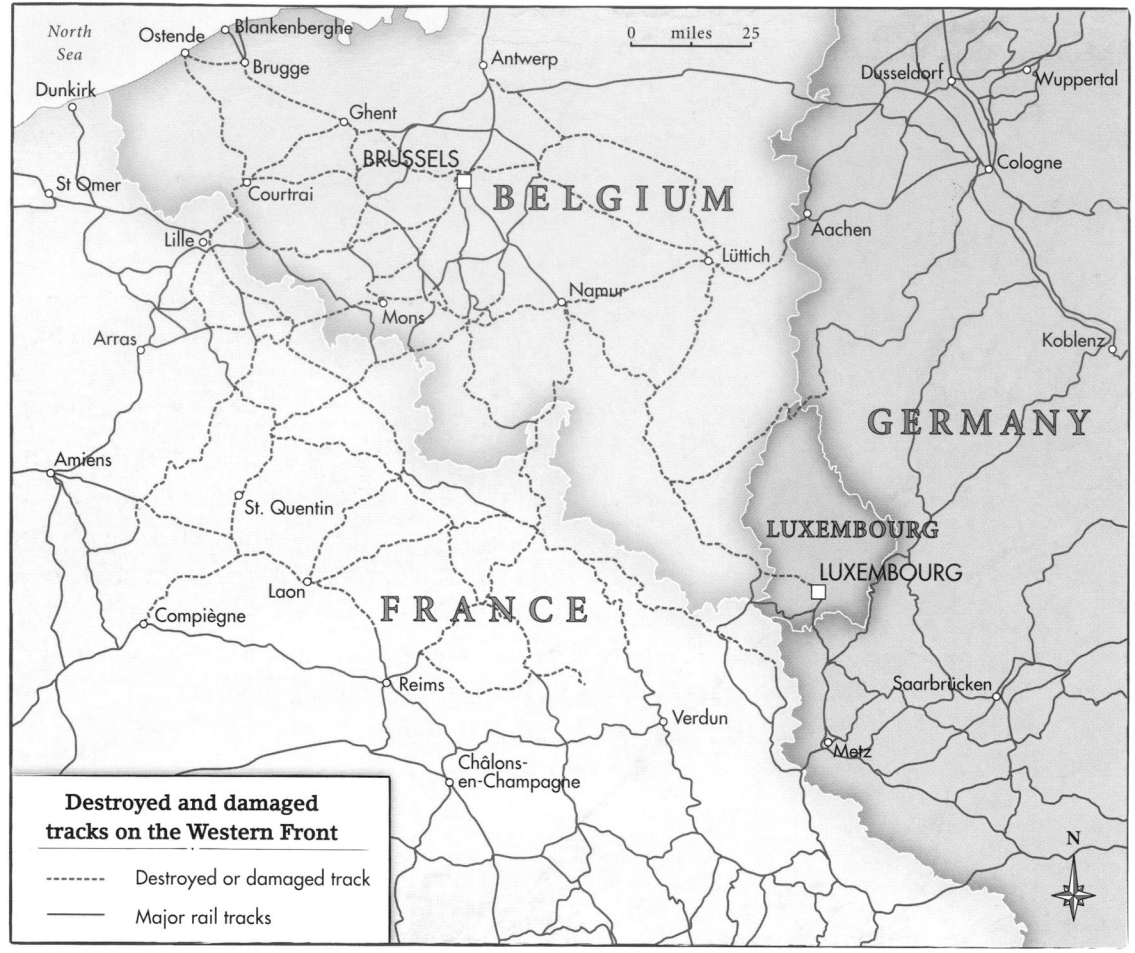

EIGHT TRAINLOADS OF IRON SENT AMOK

On Saturday night eight trains heavily laden with iron ore were sent out from Antwerp at full speed, the drivers jumping off the footplates just in time.

The trains were sent in the direction of Louvain. What happened is not known, but the idea is that they must have been wrecked at some point, and that the track would be damaged, so hindering German operations.

By the time these brave acts were being reported, the Belgian army and government had retreated to the city of Antwerp, where, sheltering behind its ring of fortresses, they were making a last-ditch effort to

LEFT A German map giving an overview of the western theatre of war – the red lines indicate the areas of track that needed repair.

BELOW Some of the trains deliberately derailed by retreating Belgian troops.

hold out against the Germans. By October, even that last stronghold had fallen, and almost the whole of Belgium was occupied.

Overall, the impact of railway resistance remains open to debate. Clearly, it was not enough to protect Belgium. Nor does it seem to have significantly slowed the Germans' advance in the short term – by early September they were within thirty miles of Paris. However, some historians argue that railway sabotage, as part of Belgium's broader resistance, bought France and Britain time to organize their response. Others stress the fact that, as the advance continued, railway damage limited Germany's options for moving men and materiel. Some contend that this lack of flexibility fatally undermined the Schlieffen-Moltke Plan, contributing to its ultimate failure and the onset of stalemate in the trenches. Whatever the truth, Belgian railway sabotage proved the lengths to which the country was prepared to go in the name of neutrality. In Britain, pledged to protect that neutrality, it helped convince those in charge to honour their promise. On 4 August, as Belgium's railway tunnel bombs were being detonated, Britain demanded that Germany desist from invading. Germany refused and, with that, Britain declared war. The world's greatest empire had entered the fray.

MOBILIZATION – THE BRITISH EXPEDITIONARY FORCE TAKES TO THE TRACKS

Within days, the order had been given for the British Expeditionary Force to join the fighting, and Britain's railways were being put through their paces as tens of thousands of men were dispatched to the Continent.

Writing in the immediate aftermath of the conflict, Edwin Pratt – probably the first historian of the railways and the Great War – claimed the mobilization of the British Expeditionary Force as a triumph for the rail industry:

ABOVE German soldiers marching through the Place Charles Rogier in Brussels in August 1914.

Supposing that the British railway companies had not devoted so much attention as they had done to the preparation of their Emergency Time-tables . . . that they had shared in the unpreparedness which, rightly or wrongly, was attributed to the country as a whole; that, in consequence thereof, the attempt to carry out the mobilisation and the embarkation of an Expeditionary Force at so short a notice had either led to chaos or been attended by serious delay in the arrival of that Force on the other side of the Channel; what would have been the probable result of such conditions? Would it still have been possible to 'roll back the invader' and to save France, if not, also, to save Europe, by the end of November, 1914?

While his contention that Britain's railways saved Europe might be overblown, most historians agree that the system coped admirably with its first wartime challenge, thanks to careful pre-war planning and ruthlessly efficient execution.

The architect of the mobilization plans was the colourful character Sir Henry Wilson, who took up the post of Director of Military Operations for the War Office in 1910. A lifelong Francophile, Wilson had long been convinced that Britain might need to intervene in a Continental war between France and Germany. He spent summer holidays exploring the Franco-German border by train and bicycle, observing German strategic railway building at first hand, and back home he ran war games to try to predict how a conflict between the Great Powers would unfold.

Wilson was shocked at Britain's lack of preparation for a Continental campaign. Although there was an embryonic 'With France' scheme worked out, he described it in his diaries as a 'pure academic, paper arrangement of no earthly value to anyone'. Wilson set himself the challenge of getting Britain battle-ready. Liaising closely with the French, he firmed up the strategy. In the event of a German invasion via Belgium, British troops would cross to Le Havre via Southampton, from where French trains would carry them towards the fighting.

RIGHT General Sir Henry Wilson, Director of Military Operations, whose commitment to military planning led him to spend holidays reconnoitring the European countryside.

The lynchpin of Wilson's plans was an elaborate series of railway timetables for bringing the six divisions of the British Expeditionary Force to Southampton. Drawn up in secrecy, they were the product of two years of work and provided for the arrival and unloading of seventy trains per day at the harbour. To coordinate the process, Wilson's team enlisted the help of the London and South Western Railway Company, which ran the lines serving Southampton. As 'secretary company', the London and South Western liaised between the War Office and the other railway companies to work out exactly which connections each train would need to make in order to arrive at Southampton on time for embarkation.

When the moment arrived to put the plans into action, the railway companies faced some unforeseen challenges. For a start, the crunch came on a bank-holiday weekend, and the network was heaving with pleasure-seekers enjoying the break. What was more, many of the

BELOW Troops packed onto ships embarking at Southampton.

territorial troops had departed for summer training camps. With the nation on war alert, they had to be returned to their bases, and the railways were put under further strain as arrangements were quickly improvised. Edwin Pratt describes how, for example, Welsh railways had to coordinate transporting 9,000 servicemen back to their depots in just 24 hours, conjuring up 27 trains to complete the task.

Politicians put a further spanner in the works, first prevaricating over whether to send a force to the Continent at all, and then deciding to hold back two of the six divisions of the British Expeditionary Force, meaning the carefully conceived plans had to be extensively reworked at the last minute.

The biggest challenge was always going to be orchestrating the epic operation at Southampton. Amazingly, here, the railway and military authorities not only hit their ambitious targets but exceeded them. Only one train arrived late, and that by only a few minutes; most other services turned up ahead of schedule. Every twelve minutes on average, a full troop train arrived at the docks. It took just fifteen minutes to unload its cargo – which included not just men but horses, weapons and supplies – and within forty minutes of having entered the dock the empty train would be on its way out again.

Historian Ian Beckett has analysed the official statistics to reveal the true extent of Southampton's success story. In the event, the docks handled not seventy trains a day but ninety. By 26 August, 65,814 men had been sent to France. The process was so swift that the first troops were ready for action before the German authorities even realized they had landed on the Continent.

Of course, disembarkation at Le Havre was not the end of the journey. The final stage of deployment – transporting the troops to the railhead from which they would join the fighting – was more difficult to coordinate. In the run-up to war, the French and British military had cooperated on exercises, practising working together to load British troops onto French trains, but with no firm commitment from Britain to send troops, plans were not set in stone. The French couldn't be sure how many vehicles would be needed, or when, but in the end managed to cobble together 361 trains, which carried 115,000 men and 46,000 horses to the Belgian border.

For the British soldiers, this part of the journey was a leap into the unknown. As they boarded unfamiliar wagons, surrounded by strange

LEFT Michael Portillo
at Southampton,
consulting the
1909 Field Service
Regulations, which
define mobilization as
'the process by which
an armed force passes
from a peace to a
war footing, that is to
say its completion to
war establishment in
personnel, transport
and animals'.

sights and sounds, they couldn't imagine that this was to be the start of
a military campaign unlike any they had seen before. Among the men
of the British Expeditionary Force was Private Edward Roe of the East
Lancashire Regiment, whose diaries were preserved after the war and
published in 2004. The entries for 23 and 24 August 1914 describe his
first taste of French rail travel:

> *[23 August] Some secured carriages with 'Hommes' written on
> them, others were manoeuvred into trucks or boxes labelled
> 'Chevals'. We all 'Hurrahed' when the train kicked off: war for a
> certainty at last . . .*

> *[24 August] On the way to the frontier, or wherever we were going,
> I noticed in several instances that women were working in the
> signal boxes instead of men, owing to the men being called to the
> colours . . . Every station presented the appearance of hurry and
> bustle owing to the enormous amount of war material and troops
> proceeding to the fighting area. At every station old men in greasy
> peak caps and dressed in blue reefer jackets shouted instructions
> to us in French, which we do not understand.*

So began the experience of the first British men to fight in the First World War. By the end of the year a third of the soldiers whom the railways had so efficiently brought to France would be dead. But for now the unfamiliar French locomotives were pulling Private Roe and his comrades towards the battlefield, where the first engagement with the enemy was already under way.

BATTLE OF THE MARNE – RAILWAYS AND THE WAR OF MOVEMENT

On 23 August, at Mons in Belgium, British troops clashed with the Germans for the first time. The Battle of Mons saw a small but efficient British force pitted against a German contingent almost three times its size. Despite the Germans' numerical advantage, the British Expeditionary Force put up a good fight. They were highly trained professional soldiers, whereas many of their German opponents were conscripts. Apparently, the British rifle rounds were so rapid that the Germans mistook them for machine-gun fire. One officer's brave defence of a vital railway bridge over the Mons-Condé canal cost him his life but won him the war's first Victoria Cross. For most of the day the British held out against their attackers, but eventually they were forced to withdraw back over the French border.

It was a pattern being repeated all along France's north-eastern frontier that August, as French troops similarly tried and failed to repel the German army's advance. This early phase of the fighting was a war of movement – utterly unlike the static trench warfare to follow. Cavalry reconnaissance parties galloped across the landscape. Vast armies of foot soldiers were on the move. Rival forces marched boldly towards one another through field and city, to engage in open battle where they met.

On both sides, the military leaders had to make split-second strategic decisions, reacting to the rapidly changing situation on the ground. As they tried to second-guess each other's next move, they anxiously scrutinized the railway maps. Misjudge where next to send their troops and they risked defeat.

During the last days of August, the French and British armies retreated in the direction of Paris, with German forces hard on their heels. For the

OVERLEAF British troops arriving in France. By the end of 1914, a third of those delivered in the first wave of mobilization had lost their lives.

men of the British Expeditionary Force, the retreat from Mons was a gruelling ordeal. For two weeks they marched almost non-stop, pausing only to fend off their attackers. At Le Cateau, 55,000 British soldiers stopped to fight 140,000 Germans at a cost of almost 8,000 casualties. Then the relentless retreat continued. By the end of the fortnight, the men's feet were bloodied, their uniforms in tatters. Many of them had walked more than 200 miles.

Meanwhile, the Germans were making good progress on their planned route through Belgium and France. It seemed they had the upper hand, but this war of movement was stretching their mighty military machine to the limit. As the infantry advanced on foot, the railway troops behind them needed to follow closely, securing the vital rail routes that would keep the army fed and supplied. Motor vehicles were in short supply, so the final link in the supply chain was horse-drawn transport. Unless the front line remained within manageable distance of the railhead, food and equipment simply couldn't reach the men in the field, and the invasion would stall.

The very speed of the German advance meant they risked outpacing their railways. As August wore on, the infantry got further and further from their railheads. Historian of military logistics Martin van Creveld has shown that at one point in early September the Second Army was over 100 miles away from the nearest railway depot. To a certain extent the men were able to get round this problem by improvising, requisitioning food from the towns and villages they passed through. But soon their horses were getting sick from a lack of suitable fodder, and it was becoming harder and harder for all the apparatus of modern war to keep pace with the troops.

What was more, the sheer ambition of the Schlieffen-Moltke Plan was taking its toll. To reach Paris in accordance with the schedule, the northernmost First Army had to march for huge distances. Amazingly, its men covered over 300 miles in the space of a month. But, like the British and the French, the German infantry were exhausted, and it wasn't clear how much longer they could keep it up.

Just how many more days the Germans could have sustained their relentless forward momentum we will never know, because the situation was about to change. Dismayed by the German advance, the leader of the French army decided to act. And to help him turn the situation around, he placed his faith in the railways.

GEN. JOFFRE GIVING ORDERS   3209-11

ABOVE General Joffre giving orders in the field. The French railways were vital to his bid to arrest the German advance.

French Commander in Chief Joseph Joffre had helped shape France's pre-war plans, which provided for a flexible deployment of troops, depending on the location of the threat. But when the German invasion began, Joffre misjudged the route of the force coming through Belgium and sent the bulk of his troops too far south.

Combined with other tactical mistakes, this strategy proved disastrous. Defeat piled on defeat, and, as August wore on, Joffre resolved on a change of approach. He reviewed tactics on the battlefield, issuing stern instructions for the artillery and infantry to work better together. He shook up the army leadership, sacking generals who weren't helping his cause. And, crucially, he decided to regroup his forces. Joffre envisaged a new army, created by bringing reinforcements from the German border zone back towards the area north of Paris. From there they would be ready to help launch a fresh attack on the invaders.

The railways were crucial to achieving this vision. Luckily for Joffre, the French system worked in his favour. The network was centred on Paris, with main lines radiating out towards the provinces. Within the city, these were linked by a kind of railway ring road called the Grande Ceinture (Grand Belt), enabling troops to transfer smoothly between the key arteries. Between the capital and the Franco-German border, many additional east–west lines had been built in the pre-war years, with further north–south tracks added to connect up the spokes.

It all added up to a remarkably flexible system for moving men around the battle zone. And Joffre showed just what it could do, putting the railways into action to assemble his new army. Between 27 August and 2 September, over around 200 trainloads of troops chugged westwards. Meanwhile, the Germans were making some decisions of their own. While Joffre was using the railways to bolster his forces in the area around Paris, in contrast his German conterpart, Helmuth von Moltke the Younger, was weakening his forces in the critical sector by sending men eastwards to help battle the Russians. This left his forward line in France spread dangerously thin.

ABOVE Reservists at Gare de l'Est, Paris, 1914.

LEFT Trains could only carry troops so far. From the railheads, these French soldiers would have had to march, laden with kit.

Then, fatefully, Moltke decided to abandon one of the key principles of Schlieffen's pre-war plans – the grand sweep round the north-west of Paris. Believing that the French and British were almost beaten, his westernmost troops swung southwards, with the intention of passing to the east of the capital. The aim was to draw this phase of fighting to a speedy conclusion by rapidly rounding up the flagging Allies.

But this change of plan provided the newly invigorated French army with the opportunity it had been waiting for. Joffre's new army gathered in the capital, ready to attack the German flank as it passed. When the two sides finally met on 5 September, the French took the Germans by surprise, and the series of battles that ensued is now remembered as the Battle of the Marne.

Joined by the exhausted remnants of the British Expeditionary Force, for the first time the French succeeded in checking the Germans' progress. Moltke's troops were forced to retreat, backtracking as far as the river Aisne. However, this breakthrough was far from

BELOW German troops en route to Russia.

a decisive victory for the Allies. At the Aisne, the Germans dug in, building trenches to protect their position. The Allies attempted another offensive but failed to overcome the German defences. It seemed deadlock had been reached. But the war of movement wasn't quite finished.

BELOW Wounded soldiers arrive at Chalons-sur-Marne in October 1914.

Using the railways, both sides began a desperate race to the north. Ian Beckett has calculated that between 14 September and 17 November 800,000 Allied troops were transported through France and Flanders in some 6,000 movements. The two sides were trying to outflank each other, but neither force was able to move fast enough to gain the advantage.

LEFT French
reinforcements
in Dunkirk.

BOTTOM LEFT German
military personnel
in a trench.

BELOW French infantry
firing from a trench.

As they moved towards the Channel, fighting as they went, the lines of trenches extended behind them until by November they had reached the sea.

The first phase of the railway war was over. The Western Front was born. Two parallel rows of trenches, separated by 'no-man's-land', stretched for 475 miles from the Belgian coast to Switzerland. They marked a frontier that was to move no more than a few miles in either direction for almost four years. Behind the line, the Germans now controlled a railway system that stretched from the vital French junction of Lille back through Belgium and Luxembourg into Germany. On the Allied side, Amiens held the key to the Channel ports and thence back to Britain. Soon, the Front's insatiable hunger for men, machinery and supplies was to usher in a new era in British railway history.

CHAPTER 2

RISING TO THE CHALLENGE

Britain's railways were at their peak in 1914, with 178 railway companies running services on around 20,000 miles of track. Alongside their locomotives, carriages, stations and workshops they owned and operated dockyards and steamships, warehouses and motor vehicles.

Immediately war was declared, the state seized control of most of the network as planned. The experienced railway managers who had sat on the Railway Executive Committee since 1912 were now going to ensure that Britain's fiercely competitive railway companies would work in harmony, coordinating massive movements of men, machinery and supplies. It was time for the railways to do their bit.

ANSWERING THE CALL – THE NORTH EASTERN RAILWAY PALS

BELOW The famous First World War poster featuring Lord Kitchener, used to recruit his 'New Army'.

With the outbreak of war, Britain faced a manpower crisis. Compared to the vast armies of France, Germany and Russia, millions strong, British forces were tiny. There were just 247,000 troops in the regular army. Even adding in the reserves and territorials put the total at under 750,000 men. A 'New Army' was needed. But the authorities were reluctant to force conscription on the nation. Instead, recruiters launched a hard-hitting campaign in a bid to raise thousands of volunteers. As an enticement, they gave men the chance to join up with their friends, colleagues and neighbours in so-called 'Pals' battalions. The idea was a resounding success, with many battalions able to fill their ranks several times over. Most Pals came from the same town or city, but there were also battalions of footballers, stockbrokers, public-school alumni and, thanks to the North Eastern Railway Company (NER), one composed solely of railwaymen.

The railways were the backbone of Britain, and their skilled workforce of more than half a million men was a rich reserve of potential military talent. The North Eastern was one of the giants of the railway age, by the eve of the war boasting a network that reached from East Yorkshire up to the Scottish border, and revenues of over £12 million a year. In its locomotive sheds and stations, its warehouses and back offices, the NER had over 50,000 male employees.

Within days of the declaration of war, 2,000 North Eastern railwaymen had signed up for service. Then, in September 1914, the NER's managers took the bold step of offering employees the chance to serve together in a specially formed North Eastern Railway Pals Battalion. As an added incentive, they promised to keep volunteers' jobs open for the duration of the war, provide for their families and keep up their pension contributions. In order to form the battalion, 1,100 recruits were needed but, amazingly, 3,000 employees answered the call.

The new battalion was named the 17th Northumberland Fusiliers, and the railway company offered up warehouse space in its newly built King George Docks at Hull for the housing and training of the new

recruits. A 1926 history of the Railway Pals, *A Record of the 17th and 32nd Battalions Northumberland Fusiliers, 1914–1919,* by Lieutenant-Colonel Shakespear, whose battalion served alongside them on the Western Front, draws on diary entries to tell the men's story. It's clear that for the NER's porters, station masters, firemen and ticket collectors, the new daily schedule took some getting used to:

ABOVE The Railway Pals training at King George Docks, Hull.

> *Reveille 5.30 a.m., half-hour's doubling, breakfast, musketry, platoon drill, bayonet fighting, physical exercise, dinner, visual training, section drill, then finish. Sometimes we had lectures at night. The physical training was under an Aldershot instructor, nicknamed the 'India Rubber man', a regular 'terror'. He certainly did us good, but he made us sweat profusely.*

Initial training complete, to their surprise the troops were posted not to France but to East Yorkshire. In this early stage of the war there was a very real threat that Germany might attack Britain's east coast, and the battalion was dispatched to help defend the area around Easington and Kilnsea. On 16 December 1914, these fears were realized when German ships off the coast shelled Hartlepool, Whitby and Scarborough, killing over 150 people and causing huge damage to buildings. Among the dead were four employees of the NER and one ex-employee, serving with the Durham Pals, though luckily the 17th Northumberland Fusiliers escaped unscathed.

While in Yorkshire, the railwaymen's duties included building trenches, a task that came naturally to many, thanks to their engineering experience. The Railway Pals' skill so impressed their superiors that it was decided to make the 17th Northumberland Fusiliers a so-called 'Pioneer' battalion, responsible for building and maintaining the vital infrastructure that supported their comrades. Alongside ordinary infantry duties, Pioneers dug and drained trenches and built supply roads. They were also often responsible for maintaining one of the war's brutal innovations – the barbed-wire defences that scarred the battlefield and inflicted vicious injuries on those who ventured into no-man's-land.

By November 1915, the battalion's full training was complete, and the men crossed the Channel to France. Like so many of the Pals battalions, their destination was the Somme valley, where the men were to get their first real taste of life at the Front. Conditions in billets were a far cry from the familiar comfort of the NER ticket office or the locomotive shed, and the men's diaries describe close encounters with mice and worse. Even the simple act of bathing was an ordeal at the Front:

RIGHT Some of the 17th Battalion Northumberland Fusiliers receiving rations at a billet.

The baths were in a house and were of the 'everything-at-the-double' kind . . . having undressed, all our clothes were hung on a peg. Suddenly a trap door opened in the ceiling, and clothes, peg and all, disappeared. This caused us no little consternation, but it appeared they were only going to be fumigated. We had to run in our birthday suits into a big concrete-floored room, hop into a tub, spend about two minutes in it, out, and into another room to dry ourselves, and then out into the garden and upstairs into a loft, where we found our clothes waiting. The whole business occupied about ten minutes, and it was decidedly funny to see a file of naked men running from one room to another, spurred on by the bath attendant shouting ''alf a minute to go,' with a pronounced Cockney accent.

The Railway Pioneers had been sent to the Somme to help prepare for a major offensive planned for the summer. For the first half of 1916, the battalion was kept busy building roads and railways in readiness for the big push, but the young men from the NER still found time for rest and relaxation. Their diaries mix accounts of hard work and tough conditions with memories of *steak-frites* in French cafés and high jinks on St George's Day, which included the spectacle of soldiers wrestling whilst bareback mule riding. It was the calm before the storm, for July of that year would bring the Pals face to face with death on an industrial scale.

RIGHT Private F. Bays featured in the *North Eastern Railway Magazine* alongside other fallen NER railwaymen.

The Battle of the Somme was intended as an overwhelming attack that would force back the German lines, breaking the stalemate of trench warfare and relieving the French, who had been bearing the brunt of the fighting at Verdun. The Pioneers were to play a crucial role, following behind the advance and digging new trenches in order to keep open the lines of communication. A few days before the planned offensive, their diary entries as recorded by Shakespear bear witness to the preliminary bombardment of the German lines:

It is tremendous, it is awful, but it is glorious, because it is ours. Six months ago, had you told us such a bombardment by the British Army was possible, we would not have believed you; had you told Fritz, he would probably have laughed. We can hear the short, sharp bark of the eighteen-pounders, constant, always, like the roll of a drum, then the deeper boom of the 'hows' but a little behind in the rapidity of their fire, and then, over our heads, the swish of the heavy shells from some great monster, either on the railway or behind in the woods.

This barrage was intended to destroy the German defences, making the attack quite literally a walkover. But when the assault finally came, on 1 July 1916, it proved to be a bloodbath. On the first day alone, overall British casualties were estimated at 57,000, of which over 19,000 were killed. Many of these were Pals, newly arrived in France, fresh from training. As wave after wave of men went over the top to face the onslaught of shells and bullets, the NER battalion's work was hindered by the bodies of the dead and injured that clogged the existing trenches. Yet against the odds, the Railway Pioneers succeeded in opening up new ones that reached the German lines.

Amazingly, despite working under constant fire, the Railway Pals' losses were relatively modest. After the intense fighting of the first sixteen days of the battle, just ten men of the battalion had been killed, eighty-

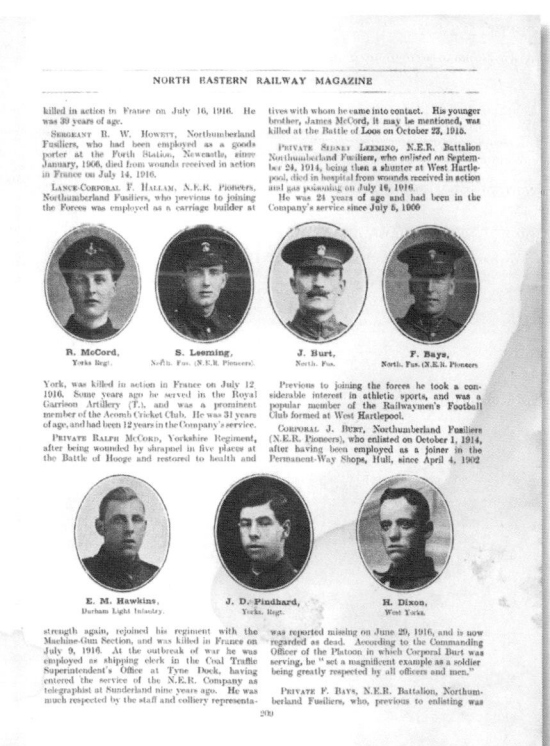

six wounded and one was missing. Still, every one of those deaths was keenly felt back home in the north-east of England. The *North Eastern Railway Magazine* published details of all the employees killed in action. Among those commemorated in its September 1916 edition was twenty-seven-year-old Private F. Bays, 'who, previous to enlisting, was employed as a wagon builder at York', with four brothers in the Army, 'three of them being at the front'. Also remembered was Private Sidney Leeming. 'A popular member of the Railwaymen's Football Club formed at West Hartlepool', this former shunter 'died in hospital from wounds received in action and gas poisoning on July 16, 1916'. The magazine is a sobering reminder that these victims of the Somme weren't professional soldiers but sons, husbands, brothers and, of course, dedicated railwaymen.

Intended as a short, sharp, shock, the Somme campaign actually dragged on into the autumn. And it became clear that the railway supply network was hopelessly inadequate for the task before it. New men were constantly being brought in to replace the dead and wounded, and unprecedented quantities of supplies were required. The railways that fed the front line needed a complete overhaul, and to help achieve it the NER Pioneers were converted to a railway battalion. In the words of the author of the battalion history: 'no better selection could have been made, for no battalion of the British Army contained more railway experts'. From now to the end of the war, railway work was to be the NER Pals' main occupation.

LEFT The Pals' platelaying experience proved invaluable at the Front.

In 1917, their work was to take them to Flanders and the Ypres Salient, where the British and Canadian front line bulged into German territory, leaving the Allied forces vulnerable on three sides. Here, the men of the 17th Northumberland Fusiliers were tasked with building a new railway, intended to bolster supply lines prior to another major offensive. The 'Great Midland Railway' was one of the Railway Pals' greatest triumphs. Its route crossed the Yser canal, just 1,800 yards from the front line, and to fill the canal the men worked in shifts from 4 a.m. to 10.30 p.m., each carting 150 barrows of earth per day, often under heavy fire.

Their efforts were part of the preparations for what became the

infamous Battle of Passchendaele. Described by A. J. P. Taylor as 'the
blindest slaughter of a blind war', still today the battle conjures up
images of helpless men mired in Flanders mud. In these conditions,
the Railway Pals were tasked with building light railways as fast as the
advance would permit, at one point laying 16 feet a minute for a whole
2,600-foot stretch in order to provide the gunners with shells by train as
quickly as possible.

When the tide finally turned in the Allies' favour in summer 1918,
the Railway Pioneers were there, supporting the final advance by
cutting trenches and building roads and artillery tracks. By November

the battalion had reached Belgium, where German resistance gradually tailed off to nothing. But, surprisingly, the battalion's official war diary contains no entry at all for 11 November. A personal diary extract reproduced by Shakespear explains: 'when the company was in Péruwelz another division passed through, and a rumour was started about there being an Armistice proposed. It was not until the 12th November that we had official information that hostilities had ceased.'

By mid 1919, the battalion had been demobilized, and the men returned home, often to take up their old jobs on the railway. Many of Britain's Pals battalions were not so lucky – a good number were disbanded before the war finished, so great were their losses. Over the course of the conflict, the battalion had seen sixty-seven men killed in action, with thirty-eight more dying from their injuries, four from gas and three from sickness. Today, their names are commemorated on the North Eastern Railway Memorial in York, designed by Sir Edwin Lutyens, which lists the 2,236 NER employees who lost their lives in the conflict.

'THE BOYS OF THE N.E.R',
AS PUBLISHED IN THE *NER MAGAZINE*

Along our line, from Hull to Tyne
And north to the Berwick wall
A signal ran
To every man,
'Do you hear your Country call?'

CHORUS:
Hurrah! Hurrah! Hurrah!
For the Boys of the N.E.R.
Who are now enrolled
In the 'Old and Bold'
And keen to go to War.

From every grade, to England's aid,
Went twice two thousand – then
A thousand more
To form a corps
Of all North Eastern men.

(CHORUS)

So here's to all who heard that call
To fight across the foam.
And here's to 'The Day'
When blithe and gay
They'll all come marching home.

(CHORUS)

AMBULANCE TRAINS

Mechanized war brought with it new and horrifying types of casualties. Machine guns, barbed wire, shellfire and poison gas inflicted horrendous injuries, and infection festered in the dank, muddy trenches. Removing the sick and wounded from these conditions was an urgent priority, and, right from the start, the railways were at the heart of the operation.

The idea of the ambulance train was born in the nineteenth century during the American Civil War, and by the turn of the twentieth century the British Army had also experimented with the idea, using specially converted carriages to transport men injured during the Anglo-Boer War of 1899–1902.

Over the next decade, as Britain contemplated the increasing likelihood of a Continental conflict, plans were made to use ambulance trains to transport the wounded from British ports to hospitals, and detailed designs for the trains were drawn up.

The day immediately following the declaration of war, a batch of twelve of these trains was ordered, and the first was ready for service just three weeks later. Built by the railway companies, they were made from converted carriages of all kinds – from standard passenger coaches to dining cars. They were designed not just for transport but for providing treatment on the go, with on-board pharmacies, kitchens, and offices for doctors and nurses.

The idea was that injured troops would be carried to the French ports on French trains, before crossing the Channel to board one of these well-equipped British medical expresses. But the French system soon began to creak under the strain of invasion. Casualties were being transported in whatever vehicles could be found, and conditions were far from ideal, as one nursing sister noted in her diary:

> *A train of cattle trucks came in from Rouen with all the wounded as they were picked up without a spot of dressing on any of their wounds, which were septic and full of straw and dirt . . . A twenty hours' journey with them in frightful smells and dirt . . . they'd been travelling already for two days.*

RIGHT Interior views of the much-heralded ambulance cars.

To address the dire need for better transport, in October 1914 the first of many British-built ambulance trains was sent to France. On 14 November 1914, the Medical Correspondent of *The Times*, who had a guided tour of the train, declared it 'probably the most perfect hospital train in the world' and provided readers with a detailed description of its state-of-the-art facilities:

> *The beds are placed against the sides of the carriage and can be lowered so as to allow free passage of stretchers up and down to the centrally placed doors. Each bed has a wire-spring mattress, a thick hair mattress, and a covering of India-rubber sheeting. The carriages are steam-heated and connected by corridors. Each carriage, too, is a unit so far as supplies of hot and cold water are concerned. The train contains a complete electric-lighting installation which can be worked at half and full light pressure, and a large kitchen; here meals for all the patients can be prepared and arrangements made for a constant supply of hot soup and beef-tea. There is, also, a well-arranged operating room . . . and a pharmacy with a complete set of drugs, dressings and other appliances.*

Articles like this were common at the time, as the propaganda machine seized on the PR potential of these all-singing all-dancing trains. But while those on the home front were reassured that Tommies in France and Flanders were being transported in the lap of luxury, the reality was rather less comfortable.

The trains were often chronically overcrowded. They frequently carried up to double the 400 patients they were designed for. Staff were regularly

ABOVE A crowded ambulance train heading for 'Blighty'.

forced to vacate their quarters to fit in more wounded men, often going without proper rest for days on end as a result. Toilet facilities were also inadequate. A letter from Sir Oliver Lyle, an officer injured in France in 1915, describes an unfortunate result of the lack of proper sanitation:

> *I had not done a pumpship since 6.0 a.m. [sic] the day before – 25 hours – and received with joy one of those miserable bottle things that the hospitals consider good substitutes for jerries. I started to pee into it & to my dismay I found it full & overflowing. I was in the top stretcher, they are arranged in three tiers, so I looked down to see the chap underneath me gazing with a fixed stare at a wet patch above him which dripped regularly down on to him. Fortunately he was a sportsman.*

Less-well-publicized features on board included padded-cell compartments, used to house those suffering from shell shock. Engineering drawings in the archive of the National Railway Museum include specifications for specially designed ashtrays, which facilitated the near-constant smoking. One former orderly later recalled that the men would spend much of their time sleeping, but at times of overwhelming pain they would reach for the 'eternal cigarette'. Nevertheless, the smell of smoke must have been preferable to the stench of unwashed men, trench foot and gangrenous wounds.

The ambulance trains were not just used by Allied soldiers. Wounded prisoners of war shared the carriages, though, perhaps surprisingly, this doesn't seem to have caused friction on board. United by their suffering, the men even extended the hand of friendship to their erstwhile foes. A former orderly described how, on one tortuous journey, a Canadian soldier who had lost his right leg offered comfort to a suffering German. With the man in obvious pain, having lost his lower jaw, he nevertheless brightened when the Canadian soldier reassured him that they were 'all in the same box'.

The vast majority of men were shipped across the Channel via Boulogne, from where they sailed to either Dover or Southampton to continue their journey by train. According to 1920s railway historian Edwin Pratt, between them these two harbour towns handled almost 2.5 million casualties on some 14,000 trains over the course of the war. Their heaviest workload came in the aftermath of the bloody Battle of the Somme, when the tally of men transported reached 10,000 in a single day. Yet despite this deluge, at its best the system for transporting casualties from the battlefield to hospital beds back home was phenomenally efficient. Apparently, on 7 June 1917, men injured in battle at Messines near Ypres at dawn had arrived by ambulance train at Charing Cross station by quarter past two the same afternoon.

The beauty of the ambulance-train system was that, once disembarked and safely ensconced on board their travelling hospitals, casualties could be sent to virtually any destination in the country for their formal treatment. By the latter years of the war, men were routinely being sent to hospitals in Scotland, far from the Channel ports. Combined with Britain's Victorian railway network, whose tentacles reached into almost every village in the land, ambulance trains helped bring about the proliferation of improvised hospitals during the war. Aristocrats offered their ancestral homes, Oxbridge colleges gave up their quadrangles, and cottage hospitals were transformed into military facilities.

This remarkable flexibility also enabled men to be sent to specialist centres such as Craiglockhart psychiatric hospital in Edinburgh, which treated victims of shell shock, or what was then the Queen's Hospital in Sidcup, which pioneered plastic-surgery techniques to reconstruct soldiers' shrapnel-ravaged faces. These advanced treatments, born out of the war, went on to help transform medicine later in the twentieth century.

But while the hospital trains click-clacked over the tracks on their merciful mission, other trains running along the very same lines were adding to the tally of destruction. For the railways moved the munitions that fuelled industrial warfare. It was a task that taxed them to their limit.

THE MAIN SUPPLY – MANUFACTURING AND MOVING MUNITIONS

All along the deadlocked Western Front, two heavily defended lines faced each other across no-man's-land. Thanks to the railway lines that kept them supplied, the armies were able to dig in for the long haul, entrenched behind walls of barbed wire. For both sides, their only chance of breaking through lay with firepower, and in the First World War that meant artillery – mortars, guns and howitzers, firing shells filled with shrapnel or explosives.

This was not entirely new military technology. But the unprecedented scale of its use, and the widespread terror it wrought, made the shell the iconic weapon of the conflict. Shellfire is believed to have caused more than half of military deaths, while 'shell-shock' victims haunted the home front, a reminder of the unseen horrors abroad. Yet, when the conflict broke out, Britain's leaders were unprepared for the leading role these deadly missiles were to play.

ABOVE An artillery position showing guns, ammunition shells, sandbags and lean-tos.

Within months of hostilities starting, demand for shells had far outstripped supply. In September 1914, British guns were firing fourteen rounds a day, double what they were being supplied. By the following month they were firing seventy-six, and by the beginning of 1915 supplies were so depleted that for every twenty German shells fired, British guns could answer with just four of their own.

By 1915, the authorities could no longer keep a lid on the problem. In the wake of the failure of a British offensive at Neuve Chapelle in France,

news broke back home of the scale of the shortage. The ensuing scandal rocked the nation, and in the political fall-out the Liberals were forced to form a coalition with the Conservatives. In a desperate bid to turn the situation around, a new Ministry for Munitions was created, headed by Liberal MP David Lloyd George. His task was to kick-start a revolution in munitions production, and the railways were key to his plans.

Under the auspices of the ministry, new factories sprang up across the country. Some made explosives, most notably H.M. Gretna in Scotland, a vast new facility that eventually expanded to be nine miles in length, containing sixteen stations and criss-crossed by eighty miles of railway tracks. Other facilities forged or filled the metal shell casings. Raw materials and components were soon being moved around Britain in unprecedented quantities. The rail-transport requirements of this new national industry were immense – amazingly, munitions made up a colossal 55 per cent of all traffic passing through the Channel ports.

To manage this epic task, a special transport branch of the Ministry of Munitions was established. Its workers were responsible for everything from building new sidings to regulating the supply of wagons; from managing traffic to easing congestion at trouble spots. The ministry provided technical assistance to the factory builders, making sure rail transport was fully integrated into the manufacturing process. For example, at Banbury's 'Filling Factory No. 9' this meant building two parallel standard-gauge railway lines into the site: one bringing empty shell cases in; the other carrying filled shells out. The two sets of tracks were linked by narrow-gauge rails, which led in and out of the filling houses. Accidentally dropping a shell could have potentially deadly consequences, so the system at Banbury was designed with minimal handling in mind. The shells could be unloaded onto handcarts, trundled into the filling house, filled and trundled out again without the need for any lifting or lowering.

The railway industry also agreed to give munitions traffic priority on the national network over all but essential food deliveries. They offered reduced fares to munitions workers and even carried certain special cargoes for free – such as fruit stones and nutshells, which towards the end of the war were used to produce charcoal for gas masks. The first poison-gas attacks took place in April 1915 at the Second Battle of Ypres, and some early designs for masks used wood charcoal to filter the air. But later it was found that heating peach pits, conkers and other nuts and seeds to high temperatures created a charcoal that captured airborne pollutants much more effectively. These were enthusiastically collected by members of the public, not just in Britain but in the USA too.

But the railways' role in the munitions crisis went beyond transport. Despite the government's efforts, it was not possible to build sufficient new factories quickly enough to keep up with the conflict's insatiable demand for ammunition and other essential combat supplies.

The answer to this dilemma was staring the authorities in the face. Before the war, Britain's flourishing railway industry was the envy of the world and boasted some of the country's most sophisticated manufacturing facilities. The Great Western Railway's vast locomotive works at Swindon alone employed 11,700 skilled men; the London and North Western's Crewe, Wolverton and Earlestown operations nearly 15,000 between them. Surely these palaces of engineering could be used to help ease the munitions shortage?

The authorities went cap in hand to the railway companies, asking them to leave off all but essential construction and repairs, and to turn their facilities over to war work. The companies agreed, offering to manufacture munitions at cost price, and, according to Edwin Pratt, by 1917 the railway companies between them were turning out almost 5,000 six-inch shells every week.

Crewe works alone made approximately 100,000 six-inch high-explosive shells over the course of the conflict, and at Crewe, as in munitions factories across the land, the majority of the workers were women. With so many men lost to the forces, the male workforce was badly depleted, and there was an urgent need for new blood to fill the factories. Lloyd George called on the leading light of the women's

BELOW To produce the huge numbers of shells required by the war effort, vast quantities of materials passed through the workshops of British railway companies.

ABOVE British 'munitionettes' pause for a photo opportunity.

suffrage movement, Emmeline Pankhurst, to help him recruit his new workforce. In July 1915, she organized a rally championing 'Women's Right to Serve'. Lloyd George appeared, exhorting the attendees to do their bit: 'Without women victory will tarry, and the victory which tarries means a victory whose footprints are footprints of blood.'

Hundreds of thousands of women answered the call, and for the old hands at Crewe, their new 'munitionette' colleagues caused quite a stir, as the assistant to the Chief Engineer of the London and North Western Railway recalled in his 1920 memoir:

> *Trim in their neat attire of light twill cap and overall, with a not infrequent hint of black silk 'open-work' veiled beneath, the ladies (God bless 'em), no sooner enlisted, lost no time in adapting themselves in a remarkable manner to the exigencies of their new surroundings . . . the girls in Crewe Works showed themselves, not only amenable to reason and discipline, but became regular enthusiasts in the work on which they were engaged.*

Women soon proved their capability up and down the land. By 1917, an estimated 80 per cent of all the munitions produced had been made by munitionettes. The work was relatively well paid but dangerous. Explosions at munitions factories killed more than 200 people over the course of the war. But the chemicals the women worked with had more insidious side effects too. Trinitrotoluene, or TNT, was highly toxic. In 1916, fifty-seven deaths were ascribed to toxic jaundice caused by TNT poisoning, and more minor complaints reported by workers included loss of appetite, nausea, dermatitis and depression. But the most striking side effect of filling shells was the alarming yellow tinge it gave the workers' skin. It earned the munitionettes the nickname 'Canaries', and an account by the daughter of one of the Banbury Filling Factory's female workers claims she was born yellow as a result of her mother's work.

As well as making new shells, the railway companies also played a vital role in a kind of wartime recycling. To begin with, after they were fired, empty shell casings were left where they lay on the battlefield; however, as the war dragged on it was realized that huge cost savings could be made by collecting the used cartridges in order to mend and refill them. This work became a core part of the railway companies' contribution to the war effort. An astonishing 29 million 18-pounder

RIGHT A woman making shells in one of the North Eastern Railway's workshops.

shell cases were re-formed over the course of the war, some of which were sent back and forth to the battlefield as many as six times.

Thanks to Britain's intensive munitions push, by 1918 the shell crisis was a distant memory. Despite extraordinary numbers of shells being fired in the war's final months – in just one week in late September 1918, British troops fired over 3 million rounds, some 83,000 tons' worth – when the fighting finally finished, Britain still had over 500,000 tons of shells in reserve.

This astonishing turnaround from the shortages of 1915 helped bring about the Allied victory that eventually ended the stalemate. It was a success story that couldn't have happened without the valiant efforts of the British railways. But it came at a huge cost. Before the deadlock was broken, both sides were driven to ever more drastic levels of destruction. The tracks that fed the Western Front's insatiable hunger for armaments indirectly contributed to thousands of casualties on both sides.

ABOVE Shells being transported on the British sector of the Western Front.

CREWE TRACTOR – A WARTIME INVENTION

The railway companies didn't just produce ammunition during the war years. Their top-notch engineering expertise was applied to a whole range of problems. At Crewe, under the leadership of Chief Mechanical Engineer Charles John Bowen Cooke, two fully equipped armoured trains were produced, and the locomotive works' cutting-edge machinery, designed for making steam engines, was put to work forging parts for guns. But perhaps the most unusual innovation to come out of the works during the war years was the so-called 'Crewe Tractor'.

The story goes that this remarkable vehicle was the brainchild of Bowen Cooke's daughter. Meeting a soldier on leave in Paris, she heard of the difficulties the men faced moving around on the front line, where the muddy ground, pitted with shell holes, was fraught with danger. What the troops needed was a new, versatile, lightweight form of transport, adaptable to the challenging conditions of the trenches, and Miss Cooke believed she had the answer.

Her idea was to build a hybrid vehicle, half locomotive, half automobile. She envisaged a Model T Ford specially adapted to run on the light railways that served the trenches. The men could drive by road as far as was practical, taking advantage of the flexibility of motor

RIGHT A Crewe Tractor in railway mode.

transport, before removing the road wheels and converting the car into a light-rail tractor for the otherwise impassable terrain of the battle zone.

Back at Crewe, with the help of the works' expert technicians, this vision was made a reality. To get it right, the engineers had to experiment, even laying a test track with a one in twenty incline to put the Crewe Tractor through its paces. Eventually, they came up with a workable design, and over 130 of these remarkable vehicles were produced and sent to the Front.

While it's unlikely the Crewe Tractor had a huge impact on life at the Front, its invention is a testament to the energy the railway companies put into aiding the war effort. This quirky little vehicle is a reminder that, alongside the destruction, the war unleashed creativity, inspiring engineers and scientists to new heights of innovation.

Whatever its limitations, the Crewe Tractor certainly captured the imagination of Bowen Cooke's assistant, whose memoir of the London and North Western Railway during the war contains this poetic description of the machine at work:

. . . like the hare it could speed along the high-road to any given point or locality, where quickly transformed it would, like the tortoise, commence its slower and uneven progress on a diminutive line of rails, laid haphazard across some devastated area, unballasted, lop-sided, up and down, this way and that way . . . Its immediate task accomplished, and in proportion as the exigencies of modern strategy demanded further changes of venue, off would come the little tractor from its erst-while voie-ferrée, and shodding itself anew with road wheels and rubber tyres, away along the high-road once again to its ensuing sphere of tortuous rail-activity.

THE RAILWAY BRANCH OF THE ROYAL ENGINEERS

The railways serving the munitions factories were just the first link in a supply chain that reached all the way into the trenches. On Britain's shores, responsibility for transport was shared between the government and the railway companies. While the logistics were challenging, the extensive Victorian network of tracks was mostly robust enough to cope with the task. But across the Channel, things were very different. The French railways, battered by conflict, needed constant rebuilding and repair. Shifting military priorities meant new lines were urgently needed. And the system soon struggled to cope with the immense traffic of munitions, men and supplies.

The men who took on this challenge were the railway troops of the Corps of Royal Engineers. According to their official history, over the course of the war, amid chaos, destruction and constant danger, they built and maintained over 2,500 miles of track – more than six times the length of Britain's East Coast main line between London and Edinburgh.

When the First World War began, no one could have predicted the scale of the work eventually done by the railway troops. The Royal Engineers established their first dedicated railway unit in the 1880s when they absorbed into their ranks the 2nd Cheshire Railway Volunteer Battalion, a group of part-time soldiers from the railway town of Crewe. By the early twentieth century, Royal Engineers railway troops had distinguished themselves in the Sudan, South Africa and elsewhere, but they still made up a modest proportion of the corps. In August 1914, there were just two permanent railway companies, making a total of around two hundred men, with three further companies in reserve.

Incredibly, when the British Expeditionary Force embarked for France, only one of these companies was with it. What was more, 8th Railway Company carried barely any equipment and no railway-building material. The French were determined to keep control of their own railways and had rejected offers of assistance from Britain's railway troops. Indeed, once landed in France, 8th Railway Company were apparently forbidden from undertaking any railway work.

But this situation was not to last. By September, the French authorities had to admit they needed Britain's help. On the 21st of that month, 8th

ABOVE Tracklaying practice at Longmoor.

Company began rebuilding a destroyed railway bridge. By the end of the war, the Royal Engineers would have repaired, improved or constructed 535 more.

Back home, it had quickly become apparent that the five existing railway units needed reinforcements – and fast. A recruitment campaign was hastily begun, and Britain's newly state-controlled railway companies came to the aid of the military, helping to gather together a force of volunteers. The vast majority already had railway experience, but to ply their trade on the battlefield they needed a crash course in military railways. That task was to fall to a remarkable school for military railwaymen, hidden away in the peaceful Hampshire countryside.

Just before the war, an army base near Liss in Hampshire, served by a military-built railway, had evolved into something of a training centre for railway troops. The base was Longmoor, and from 1908 the line was known as the Woolmer Instructional Military Railway. Jokingly nicknamed the 'Will It Move Railway' by the locals, this six-mile track now found itself at the heart of the Royal Engineers' railway operation.

The base and its railway facilities underwent rapid expansion. In 1914, just 750 men were sent out of Longmoor to the Front; by 1917 the figure was 6,212. Over the course of the war, some 16,000 men were trained there. The school covered all aspects of military railways, from construction methods to operation. The men learned everything from French locomotive vocabulary to techniques for destroying their own tracks to put them beyond the use of the enemy – special 'rail wreckers' were even tested at Longmoor during the war. Light railways were also part of the curriculum, with the 'Scenic Railway' – so called for its steep inclines and tight curves – built to test the recruits' skill at building, maintaining and operating narrow-gauge systems.

It wasn't just British troops who made use of the Instructional Railway. In 1915, the ranks of railway troops were swelled by the arrival of the Canadian Overseas Railway Construction Corps. Recruited from the immense coast-to-coast Canada Pacific Railway, some 500 officers and men underwent initial training at Longmoor before travelling to France to join the Royal Engineers. They were the first of many Canadian railwaymen who came to Europe to help with the war effort.

In fact, the local residents around Longmoor got used to the sound of Canadian accents, as the war years also saw members of the Canadian

BELOW The results of an exercise in railway demolition: a narrow-gauge track destroyed.

Forestry Corps set up a sawmill nearby. They had been called to Britain to help meet the front line's insatiable demand for timber – used in huge quantities to build trenches and railway wagons – and the Instructional Railway was used to transport the wood from their mill.

With its rows of huts and tents set amid beautiful rolling countryside, Longmoor must have been a gentle introduction to the railway war. But in France, this idyll was soon forgotten. Many of the men were constantly on the move, some even living on board trains, with separate wagons for accommodation and equipment. The work was hard and dirty, often carried out within range of enemy fire.

By 1917, there were over 100 railway companies working on the Western Front. The scale of their task was mind-boggling. As well as building new lines and repairing damaged ones, as the conflict wore on and the French struggled to cope with the demands on their network, the Royal Engineers took ever greater responsibility for running the trains. According to the corps history, the year 1917 saw the Railway Operating Division responsible for 330 miles of the standard-gauge network, rising to 815 miles by the end of the war.

But the railway troops' most Herculean feats came in the closing days of the conflict. When the Allies began to drive the Germans back in autumn 1918, the retreating troops destroyed the railways behind them. But to sustain the advance, an intact rail network was vital. As the railway troops battled to keep supplies flowing to their comrades, the pace of railway-building reached unprecedented heights. In the month of October, 242 miles of track were laid – a 63-mile stretch being built in a single week.

The Royal Engineers had played their part in victory. And they continued to work on the Western Front after the armistice, when the railways faced the fresh challenges of demobilization and the beginnings of reconstruction.

As for Longmoor, following the armistice it was quickly scaled down, but its story wasn't over. During the Second World War, the camp came into its own once again, growing even bigger than it had been in 1914–18. The Woolmer Instructional Railway, from 1935 renamed the Longmoor Military Railway, continued to be used to train armed-forces personnel until its eventual closure in 1969.

HAROLD RUDGARD, MILITARY RAILWAYMAN

Harold Rudgard was born in Burton upon Trent in 1884 and joined the Midland Railway in 1900 as a Pupil Engineer. He quickly worked his way up the ranks and was eventually promoted to the position of District Motive Power Superintendent, managing the work of locomotive sheds at Derby, Skipton and then Plaistow. He made sure the locomotives were kept in tip-top condition and that they were ready and waiting in time for every scheduled service.

Around 1911, Harold joined the Territorial Force, a forerunner of the modern Territorial Army, and a year later he travelled to Germany on a rather unusual business trip. According to his son Tony, ostensibly he was visiting on behalf of the Midland Railway, to learn about the mass-production techniques being pioneered at the giant Krupp locomotive works. But Krupp was also famed for arms manufacturing. While in the Ruhr, Harold witnessed first hand the vast scale of military preparations then under way, including the build-up of railway stock for military use. On returning to England, Harold related his findings not just to his railway bosses but to his Territorial Force superiors too.

As a territorial, on the outbreak of war Harold was called up immediately, to serve as a 2nd Lieutenant with his regiment, the Sherwood Foresters. Initially, his railway expertise wasn't put to use; instead, his technical skills were applied to the role of Machine Gun Officer, repairing and issuing these deadly new industrial weapons to the troops.

Harold's battalion, the 5th, first landed in France in February 1915, and he soon found himself in Flanders. That July, in fighting near Sanctuary Wood, he was wounded and gassed. Transported to a military hospital in Rouen, serendipity brought Harold comfort in the form of a familiar face. At his bedside was Mary Sutton, a Voluntary Aid Detachment nurse who Harold knew from before the war, as he had been at school with her four brothers. Over the course of his four-month stay in hospital they fell in love, and in 1916 they were married.

By the time Harold had recovered from his injuries, there was a pressing need for railwaymen to offer their talents to the war effort. Harold was seconded to the Royal Engineers, who brought him to Longmoor to help develop the training programme for the hordes of new railway recruits. There he got involved in all kinds of training, from laying new lines and building bridges, to teaching the soldiers how to re-rail trains that had come off the tracks.

By 1916, Harold's skills were desperately needed out on the Western Front, and he was posted to the Somme, where an ambitious new programme of light railways was being rolled out. As Superintendent of the 4th Army of the Somme Narrow-Gauge Railway, Harold's talents, honed over years as a Locomotive District Superintendent, really came into their own.

Harold oversaw the use of the light-railway system to deliver men, ammunition, food and materials. By day, wagons were loaded at the depots some five miles from the Front. Then, under cover of darkness, steam engines would pull the loaded wagons to within a mile or so of the trenches. For the final leg, petrol engines were used, so that no smoke or steam could be spotted by the enemy. At constant risk of attack, Harold frequently had to quickly rebuild track to circumvent shell holes – though it wasn't just the enemy who made his job difficult. Soldiers inexperienced in railway work were often tempted to drive the engines faster than the bumpy tracks would bear, and breakdown crews and equipment had to be provided all along the route to cope with the frequent derailments.

By 1918, Harold had been promoted to Lieutenant-Colonel and was put in charge of the vital repair and maintenance work being done at the light-railway workshops. The original workshop had been built at Berguette in France, but after the German Spring Offensive of 1918 this was dangerously close to the front line. Harold supervised the relocation of the workshop – lock, stock and barrel – to Beaurainville, some thirty miles away. Having accomplished this feat in just three months, Harold remained in charge there until July 1919, helping to keep vital supplies moving in the months after the armistice.

17/11/18
203, ASHBY ROAD,
BURTON-ON-TRENT.

My dear Son

I feel I cannot allow this great and wonderful week to pass without sending you a few words of hearty congratulation anent this blessed peace more. What joy it has brought to millions & millions. and we who are spared to rejoice must always keep in our hearts a place for those dear sons who nobly & cheerfully died that England may live and for those who joined up for love of the cause and are still alive — our colonial brothers allies. and particularly the Yanks. without whom. we should have eventually been beaten. I shall be pleased then that a grateful country will very shortly allow you to resume your work on the Midland

Railway who, with other Railways must start making good as soon as men & material can be allocated for civil occupations.

It would please me mightily if the M.R. applied specially for your release. as I feel if you dont soon settle down in a house of your own. with Mary. you may always want to live in Hotels or other expensive places — which are no good to a man of your limited means and bad breeding.

My best wishes for your welfare. May you have good health and deserved success in life. I am Your affectionate Father

Edward Rudgard

I am in good health thank God.

In summer 1919, his war service finally over, Harold returned home to his wife Mary and took up his post with the Midland Railway once again. By the end of his career he had risen to the position of Superintendent of Motive Power for British Railways. He retired in 1950, having given half a century of service to the railways.

RAILWAY GUNS

The railways' role in combat did not stop with delivering men and materiel to the front line – rail power was also used in the heat of battle. As all the belligerent nations sought to break the stalemate, they pinned their hopes on ever bigger and more destructive weapons, made mobile by railway technology.

Traditionally, so-called 'heavy artillery' meant static guns, used for siege warfare. Military engineers had experimented with rail-mounted artillery in the nineteenth century, starting in the American Civil War, but it was in the First World War that railway guns came of age. The first British examples were guns originally designed for coast defence, placed on improvised railway mounts to take them to the Front. But soon purpose-built railway guns were among the most fearsome weapons of the conflict.

The railway guns used by the British were 9.2-inch, 12-inch and 14-inch monsters, with a range of up to 20 miles. Mounted on their carriages these vast weapons weighed up to 248 tons and made a terrifying sight, dwarfing the men who worked them. Each gun needed a large dedicated crew to operate it, with as many as ten men needed just to ram the shell into the breech ready for firing.

RIGHT A trainload of 12-inch guns ready for the cross-Channel ferry.

To maximize the potential of these massive weapons, early twentieth-century technology was pushed to its limit, as railways came together with cutting-edge communications and the new art of flight. Specially built sections of track would bring the guns into position, usually thousands of feet behind the front line. Modern camouflage techniques were used to disguise the valuable machines from prying enemy eyes. Then, to train the firepower accurately on its target, aerial reconnaissance came into play. A plane would fly out over enemy lines, sending a message back in Morse code over wireless telegraph. This would be telephoned through to the gunners, who would take aim and fire.

The advantage of these massive artillery pieces was the ability to use overwhelming force from a distance, but they had some technical limitations. The heavier the gun, the bigger the recoil after firing. This meant that, for the heaviest of them, there was a real risk of the gun being blasted off the tracks unless the recoil could be absorbed. One way round this was to keep the barrel in line with the railway and allow the recoil to push the gun back along the track, but the downside was limited scope for adjusting the aim. Curved tracks could help with positioning, but the process of aiming remained unwieldy.

Britain's 14-inch guns weren't brought into action until 1918, when they were used as part of the Allies' big push forward on the Western Front in August of that year. Mounted on wagons nicknamed 'Boche-Buster' and 'Scene-Shifter', these systems became celebrated particularly after a visit by King George V. He was inspecting a 'Boche-Buster' at Maroeuil when a shot was fired at a German-held railway junction almost nineteen miles away. Apparently the 'King's shot', as it became known, was a success, inflicting 400 casualties and preventing the Germans from using that section of railway for the rest of the war.

Images of the 14-inch guns in action bring home the extraordinary size of these behemoths of the battlefield. Yet the British had still bigger ambitions for their railway guns. In 1918, five 18-inch rail-mounted howitzers were commissioned. These were guns of destruction on a vast scale. The 52-foot-long barrel alone weighed in at 85 tons – taken together with its mounting it weighed 250.

ABOVE Examining the only remaining 18-inch railway gun at Fort Nelson, Plymouth.

In the end, the 18-inch guns were not ready in time to be used in the First World War and were mothballed soon after the armistice. However, one of them found a new lease of life a couple of decades later when, united with 'Boche-Buster', it was sent to Kent to bolster the coast defences in case of an attempted German invasion. The Elham Valley Railway underwent substantial reinforcement work to withstand the unit's weight, and a hiding place was found in a tunnel near Bishop Park. Test firings in 1941 shook nearby villages, causing damage to local homes, but in the event the gun was never used against the enemy.

'Boche-Buster' and the other railway gun carriages were scrapped after the Second World War, as were most of the railway guns. However, one of the 1918 18-inch railway howitzer barrels survived and can now be seen in all its monstrous glory at the Royal Armouries Museum of Artillery, Fort Nelson, near Portsmouth.

The British weren't the only force to experiment with railway guns in the First World War. The Germans were famed for their mammoth rail-mounted artillery pieces, and the very biggest to see action during the conflict was the German-built Paris Gun. This 110-foot-long supergun was used in 1918 to attack the French capital. From a forest some seventy miles away, it fired shells that appeared to come from nowhere into the heart of the city. Historians believe its tactical significance was minimal, but as a means of terrifying the Parisian population it was second to none.

Indeed, it could be argued that the true value of the super-heavy railway guns lay in their propaganda power. Newsreels depicting the 'Monster Guns' in action projected a reassuring image to those on the home front. For the Tommies in the trenches too, the thought of the supersized railway back-up that lay behind them must have boosted morale.

Whatever their contribution on the battlefield, the railway guns epitomize the synergy between railways and war. But there were quieter ways in which the railways shaped the conflict. Over the four long years of fighting, behind the scenes, railways and railway workers strove to keep the war moving.

BELOW In 1940, one of the 18-inch howitzers went to the Proof and Experimental Establishment at Shoeburyness, where it was used for ballistic tests.

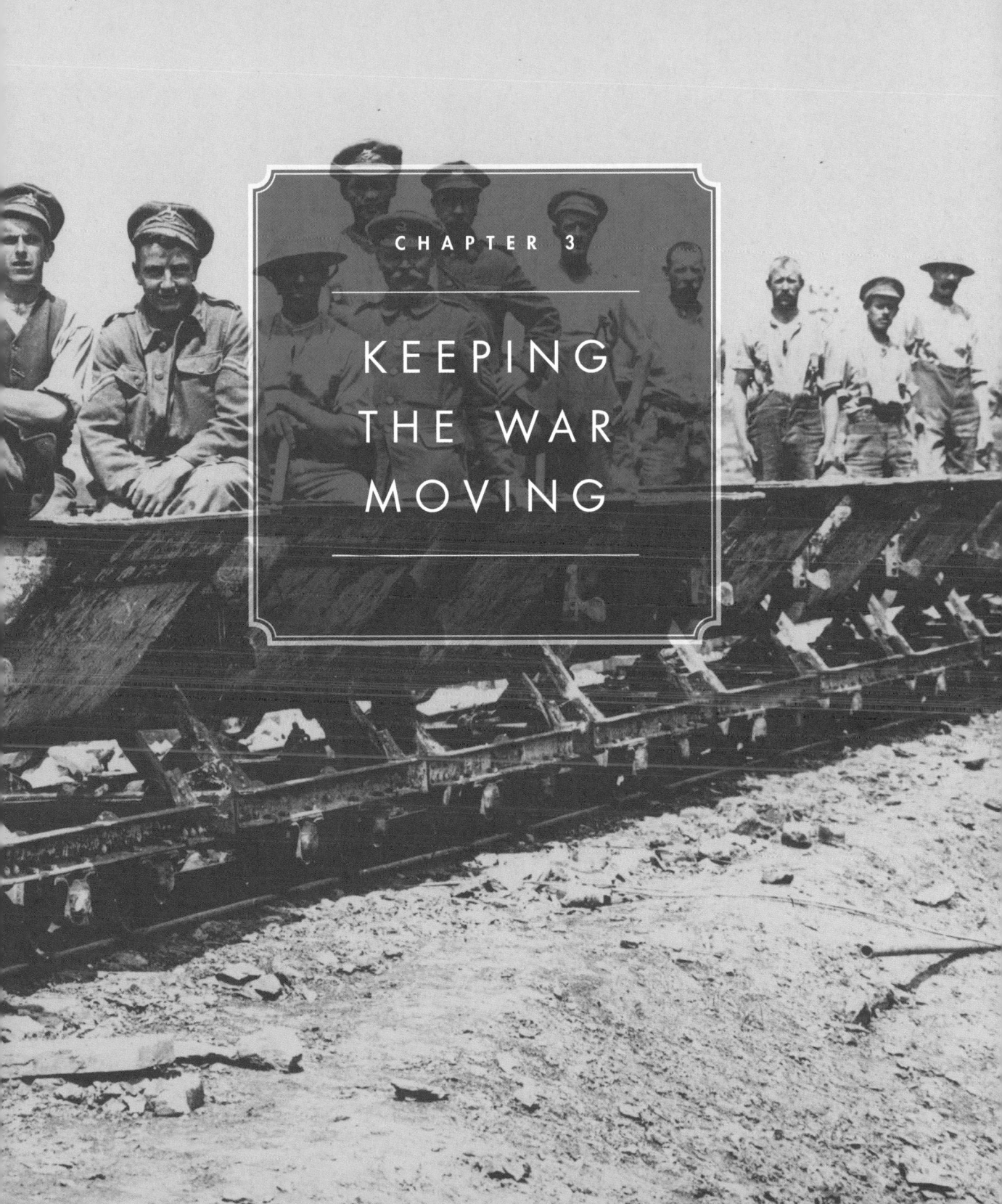

CHAPTER 3

KEEPING THE WAR MOVING

The British sector of the Western Front ran from Ypres in Belgium south into northern France. At the start of trench warfare British troops were responsible for just twenty or so miles, but by 1916 the British Front was more like eighty miles long, reaching as far south as the Somme valley in Picardy.

Before the war, the railways serving this corner of north-east France were operated by the flourishing Compagnie des chemins de fer du Nord, which ran trains out of Paris towards the Channel coast and the Belgian border. Their freight trains served the region's textile trade, thriving in cities like Lille, while passenger services carried not just locals but also tourists, including many British visitors who came to admire Picardy's stunning beaches and quaint medieval towns.

The creation of the Western Front severed this network, the front line cutting right through the main line that ran from Paris via Arras to Lille. And on the tracks that remained under French control, the tourists and textiles were replaced by huge numbers of men, horses and guns, together with all the many and varied supplies required for a twentieth-century war. By the middle years of the conflict, this heavy burden was proving too much to bear.

SIR ERIC GEDDES – FORGOTTEN HERO OF THE RAILWAY WAR

The Battle of the Somme is seared into Britain's national consciousness. Remembered as one of the darkest points in our military history, the battle has come to symbolize the futility of the First World War. More British soldiers lost their lives in its opening assault on 1 July 1916 than on any other single day before or since; yet by November troops had advanced by no more than a few miles. In many ways, this human tragedy marked the nadir of Britain's war experience. And it also revealed an uncomfortable truth: the logistical side of the British operation was at the point of collapse.

The Somme offensive placed huge demands on the Western Front's railways. Logistics historian Ian Malcolm Brown has calculated that just to supply the troops with ammunition, the number of trains needed rocketed from between five and twelve per week to between forty-five

ABOVE A damaged
German locomotive in
the Somme.

and ninety per week. Perversely, the success of drives to manufacture more munitions and recruit more men only put additional strain on the system. In the run-up to the battle, 17 new divisions – around 300,000 men – were sent to the Front, requiring almost 60 trains a week just to keep them in essential supplies.

The railways were ill-prepared for the scale of this challenge. Despite the efforts of pioneer battalions like the NER Pals, who toiled to build extra roads and railways in advance of the battle, the infrastructure in place prior to the Somme assault fell woefully short of the campaign's military ambitions. Within a few weeks of the battle beginning, the railways came close to collapse, with a tailback of around eighteen miles of trains just outside Amiens, all waiting for access to railheads to unload vital supplies.

Clearly, a radical shake-up of the system was needed. David Lloyd George – by June 1916 Secretary of State for War – knew just the man to do it. But his chosen transport tsar was neither a top bureaucrat nor a military whizz-kid. Instead, the task of transforming the railways on the Western Front fell to a grey-suited businessman. His name was

Eric Geddes, and his day job was Deputy General Manager of the North Eastern Railway.

Geddes was born to middle-class parents in India in 1875, and his biographer Keith Grieves recounts how he had his first taste of railway work as a young man in the 1890s, when he took a kind of extended gap year in the United States. During his two-and-a-half-year travels, he took on a series of blue-collar jobs, including working as a brakeman on freight trains and in a rail yard. He later worked on Indian railways before returning to Britain in 1904 to join one of the giants of the British railway industry, the North Eastern Railway, on its 'traffic apprenticeship scheme' – a fast track for managers of the future.

The NER was at that time one of the most forward-looking companies in the country, pioneering new management techniques of the kind still employed by management consultants today. Geddes soon showed a flair for this modern way of doing business, analysing company figures to sniff out cost savings and boost efficiency wherever he could. By 1911, he had risen to the rank of Deputy General Manager, second in command of the NER's multimillion-pound concern. He had been promised the top job when the General Manager retired, but the war was to take his career in an unexpected direction.

After the Ministry of Munitions was created in 1915 to tackle the critical shell shortage, Lloyd George sought out dynamic individuals from the private sector to help him in his task. He wanted men with a reputation for innovation and leadership – what he termed 'men of push and go'. In his view, industrialized warfare required the talents of captains of industry, and the railway companies were happy to offer their brightest and best minds to the war effort. Geddes was seconded to the Ministry, where he applied himself to the munitions crisis with his trademark energy and attention to detail. His work on the supply of guns and ammunition was so successful it won him a knighthood in June

1916, just before the Battle of the Somme began. When the transport crisis struck on the Western Front, Geddes was the man of the hour.

He was sent to France to conduct an investigation into all areas of transport, and his assessment was damning. In a private letter to Lloyd George, he remarked: 'This is a war of armies backed by machinery and "movement" and I do not think that "movement" has received sufficient attention.' Geddes had uncovered a lack of coordination between the different parts of the system, with railways, waterways, docks and roads all being managed by separate departments. After two years of conflict, the French railway system was battered and broken, and British support had been hopelessly inadequate – just 34 British locomotives were in operation on the Western Front, when more like 200 were needed. What equipment was there was in a bad state of repair, with few men available to maintain it. And worst of all to this man of precision and order was that the whole system was operating blind, without statistics or accurate forecasting of requirements.

Geddes was handed sweeping powers to rectify the situation. He had not one but two high-level job titles: Director-General of Transportation in France and Director-General of Military Railways. He was also made an honorary Major-General, to furnish him with the necessary authority to give orders to the armed forces. Over in France, he soon had his own HQ staffed by 100 officers and 600 clerks. Rob Langham, who has written the NER's First World War history, records how the NER workshops in York even provided him with a mobile office in the form of a specially built eight-coach train.

Never before had a civilian been given so much control over military operations. For some it was hard to stomach – the transport headquarters in France were soon wryly referred to as 'Geddesburg'. But Geddes had allies where it counted, finding a firm friend in the Commander-in-Chief of the British Expeditionary Force, General Douglas Haig. Indeed, Haig said of Geddes that he 'recognised in him the very qualities which the army in the field required'. And Geddes soon proved himself worthy of this accolade.

All the tricks of the trade Geddes had learned at the NER were brought to bear on the crisis. According to historian Chris Phillips, who has studied the railway managers' contribution to the war, Geddes behaved as if the transport system was a railway company and the armed forces its customer. His aim was to deliver the most efficient service possible

– the only difference was that success would be measured not in profit but in victory.

First, all the elements of the transport infrastructure were brought under Geddes's sole command. Henceforth, railways and roads, dockyards and canals would have to work smoothly together – just as the NER's railways and steamships, dockyards and warehouses did. One special area of focus was the ports – what use were efficient railways if vital supplies sat idle on quays for days before they were even loaded onto trains? To keep materiel moving, Geddes provided the docks with new cranes for unloading, and miles of new railway sidings were built to ease congestion.

For the first time, a forecasting system was implemented across the board. Statistics were collected and used to predict future requirements, so that the necessary locomotives, wagons and personnel could be provided in good time. Geddes put his faith in the figures, boldly ordering what he thought was needed, not what the budget dictated. He was criticized for extravagance, but Geddes believed he was simply following the same business principles he used on the NER – investing wisely to get results.

To address the drastic shortage of railway equipment in France, Geddes appealed to his former competitors back home. He asked Britain's railway companies to provide some 300 locomotives, 20,000 wagons and hundreds of miles of track. The operators did their best to comply, but the impact was felt keenly on the home front. Fares were increased and journey speeds slowed as the industry struggled with shortages. The companies even resorted to cannibalizing their own networks, earning praise from General Haig, who remarked that they 'carried their patriotism so far as to tear up from their tracks the rails that we needed'.

Historians of the railway war agree that Geddes's reforms successfully turned the crisis around. By Christmas 1917, Haig was writing in dispatches of a 50 per cent increase in railway traffic since the previous year. By 1918, it is estimated that 675 British locomotives had been sent overseas. British Railway Operating Divisions had undergone dramatic expansion and were running the trains serving the British sector, taking the heat off the overburdened French system. Extra railway troops had been recruited and hundreds of miles of light railways built. In 1916, a single offensive almost overwhelmed the transport system, but in

1917 it managed comfortably to supply four attacks at Arras, Messines, Passchendaele and Cambrai. While the strategic value of these offensives might still be open to debate, they were not hampered by logistics as the Somme had been.

Geddes's tenure was revolutionary but brief. By May 1917, he had moved on to his next challenge: supplying the Royal Navy. By the end of the war, he had reached the position of First Lord of the Admiralty – the political head of the Senior Service – with a position in the War Cabinet and, after being elected as MP for Cambridge in July 1917, a seat in Parliament.

The NER's former management trainee had come a long way. And the advent of peace didn't mark the end of Geddes's power over the railways. In 1919, the Ministry of Transport – the forerunner of today's Department for Transport – was created, with none other than Geddes as Secretary of State. High on his agenda was working out what to do about the British railways. They were still under government jurisdiction, but control was due to be handed back to the private companies. After the years of centralization, a return to the untrammelled competition of Victorian times, which had led to inefficient duplication of lines and routes, seemed like a backward step. Geddes was instrumental in steering through legislation that rationalized the system, grouping Britain's 178 pre war companies into just four giants, creating regional monopolies. This merger changed the way the railways were run for ever, sowing the seeds for nationalization after the Second World War.

His last political post saw him wield the so-called 'Geddes Axe' as Chairman of the Committee on National Expenditure, which controversially recommended swingeing cuts to balance the books after the expensive war years. Geddes eventually decided a political life wasn't for him, but he never returned to his old job with the NER. He spent the twenties and thirties working for Dunlop Rubber and Imperial Airways (the forerunner of British Airways), where he continued to demonstrate his management skills. Geddes died in 1937, just before Britain was tested by a second total war.

Geddes gave the faltering railway war on the Western Front a new lease of life at the critical moment. Thanks to him, trains went on to play an even more vital role in the conflict. Himself a product of the glory days of the Railway Age, he brought the characteristic energy and dynamism of Britain's railway companies in their heyday to a country in crisis, playing as important a role as any general. Like the generals, he wasn't always popular, and not every initiative was successful. But in the words of Lloyd George, Geddes truly was 'one of the most remarkable products of the Great War'.

LIGHT RAILWAYS – CHANGING THE WAY THE WAR MOVED

Sir Eric Geddes spearheaded a revolution in logistics. But in terms of the railways, perhaps his most radical recommendation was the wholesale adoption of a new kind of technology: light rail. From 1916, the British-held areas of the Western Front were transformed, as miniature railways began snaking their way across the trenches. In photographs, the dinky tracks and the scaled-down trains that worked them look more suited to scenic tourist trains than life in the firing line. But what these narrow-gauge railways lacked in size they more than made up for in impact. They extended the railways' reach all the way to the front line, providing the struggling Tommies with a vital artery for essential supplies. However, convincing the British Army leadership of their advantages was an uphill struggle.

BELOW A Decauville light railway moving artillery in 1906.

RIGHT The construction of a light-railway track in Champagne.

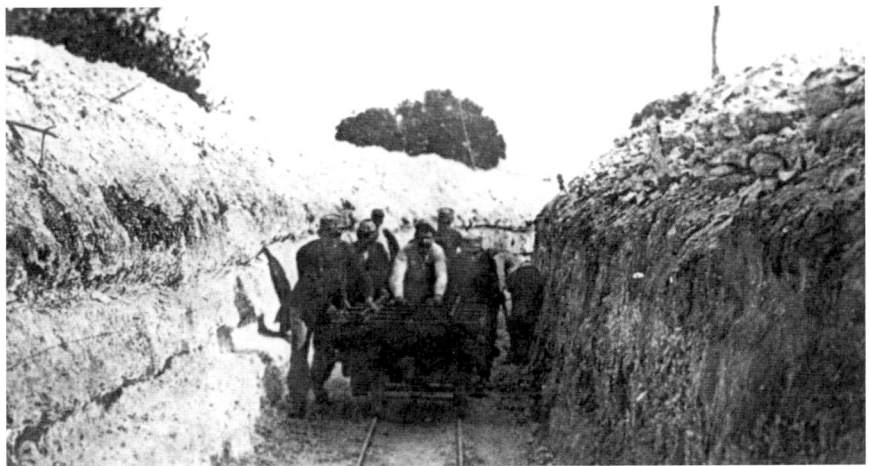

Military light rail had its origins back in the nineteenth century, thanks to a French ex-soldier and manufacturer of agricultural machinery, Paul Decauville. He invented a system of prefabricated narrow-gauge tracks, manufactured in 16-foot sections, which could be put together and taken apart rather like a train set. Requiring little time or engineering expertise to assemble, and providing a smooth route over muddy fields, it was an excellent tool for farmers, and on the Continent the armed forces were quick to spot its battlefield potential. Here was a system that provided all the advantages of rail transport, without the need for costly and time-consuming building projects. Lines could be laid quickly, then lifted and shifted as necessary, to serve the changing needs of the campaign.

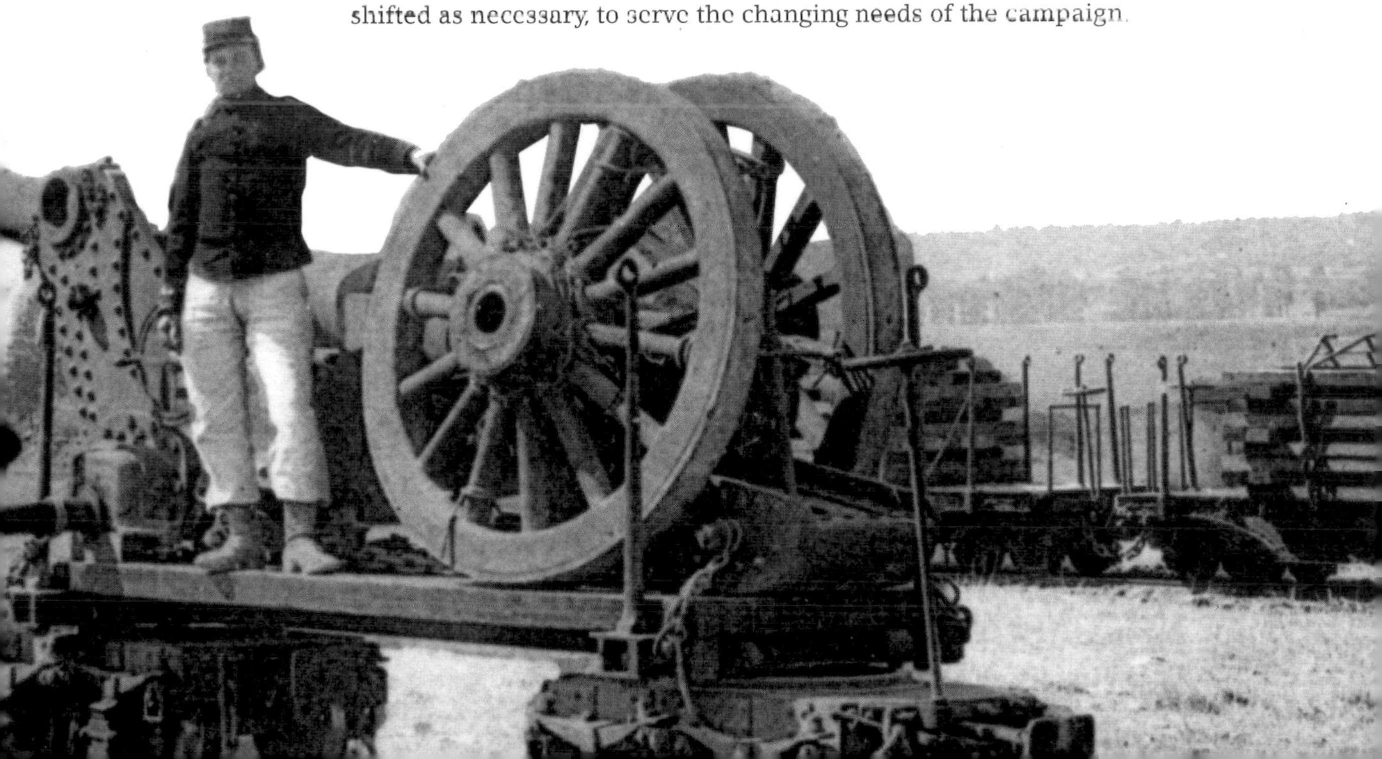

ABOVE A working party using the light railways on the Western Front.

By the eve of the First World War, France and Germany had both experimented with military light rail and were sold on its advantages. Germany, especially, had built up vast supplies of narrow-gauge material and even set up a special Feldeisenbahnabteilung (field railway section) of the army, while France had approximately 400 miles of Decauville track in store. According to railway historian Christian Wolmar, the Germans laid their first narrow-gauge tracks in Belgium within days of the outbreak of war, to help with their attack on Liège. The French weren't far behind, starting to use light railways not long after the first trenches were dug.

But in the British-controlled sectors of the Front it was a different story. The British Army believed that investing in light railways was a waste

of resources. They were convinced that soon the war would start moving again, rendering the equipment useless. They felt that motor transport, offering unparalleled flexibility, was the key to mobility beyond the railheads. In many ways this could be seen as rather forward-looking. But the planners had reckoned without the reality of trench warfare.

As the war of movement got bogged down in the trenches, the supply trucks got mired in the mud. Static warfare placed a huge burden on the country roads of France and Flanders, which soon disintegrated under the weight of the lorries, and maintaining them was a futile task. Beyond the roads, the morale-sapping job of lugging supplies through the quagmire fell to men and horses, who risked injury and even death as they navigated the waterlogged ground.

The British dabbled in light rail from 1915, getting their first real taste of its benefits when they took over a French section of the Front in February 1916. But it wasn't until Sir Eric Geddes took the reins that the British Army really put its faith in the technology. Having seen narrow-gauge rail in action during his early career in India, Geddes was in no doubt that this was the ideal way to bridge the gap between railhead and trenches.

In October 1916, he submitted a request for 1,000 miles of track and 1,000 locomotives to the War Office, and soon narrow-gauge rail began to be rolled out across the Western Front. Much of the equipment was manufactured in Britain, by companies including the Gloucester Carriage and Wagon Company and the Blake Boiler Wagon and Engineering Company of Darlington, but such was demand that locomotives were also sourced from the USA. Ultimately, over 7,000 miles of track would be ordered as light railways spread to all the theatres of war, including Africa, Mesopotamia and Palestine.

On the Western Front, the first real test of this new technology came in April 1917 with the Battle of Arras, the first major offensive attempted in the British-held sector since the Somme. Here, newly built light railways helped supply the artillery with the ammunition for a preliminary bombardment that lasted five days and used 88,000 tons of shells – around 70 per cent more than had been deployed in the Somme's opening offensive. Once troops had successfully advanced, the rapid-assembly railways were extended behind them, helping maintain hard-won positions such as the strategically vital Vimy Ridge, secured at great human cost by Canadian soldiers.

OVERLEAF Shells being loaded onto a light-railway truck for a move forward.

LEFT Light-railway
construction at
the Front.

BELOW King George
V taking a tour of
the battlefield on the
narrow-gauge railway.

Even more extraordinary than their use on the battlefield, at Arras light railways played a role in an audacious scheme to outwit the Germans. In the weeks leading up to the battle, tunnellers – mostly New Zealand troops with mining experience – created what amounted to a subterranean citadel. Existing caves beneath the city were linked up and passages extended all the way to the front line. The idea was to amass troops underground in order to launch a surprise attack. The maze of tunnels could eventually house up to 24,000 men, and had its own hospital, power station and, of course, its own light-railway system. After the Second World War, this remarkable warren was closed up and forgotten, only to be rediscovered in 1990. Today, it's home to a museum, the Wellington Quarry, where visitors can get a taste of life in the buried barracks.

By December 1917, a light-railway network of over 700 miles was in operation on the Western Front. Over 900 engines and nearly 5,000 wagons circulated in an average week, hauling 165,000 tons. The light railways were particularly successful in transporting shells, keeping the artillery supplied without the need for potentially lethal ammunition stores near the guns, but their usefulness didn't stop there. All kinds of light-railway wagons were sent to the Front. Water tanks were used to provide drinking water and also to supply locomotives; ambulance vans evacuated the wounded; and when conditions were especially muddy, the troops themselves would ride in the open wagons. King George V

himself even took to the narrow-gauge tracks on a tour of the battlefield.

The demands of light railways were different from those of the standard-gauge system. For a start, steam locomotives were far from ideal so close to the front line, as the smoke and steam acted as a beacon to the enemy. Petrol locomotives were much more suitable, but the technology was still in its infancy. A petrol-powered prototype had been designed before the war but received little attention; now, hundreds of the engines were hastily ordered.

It was the first time internal combustion had been used on any scale on the rails, and the technology soon proved its worth. Not only were the engines lighter, cleaner and quieter, they could be started instantly – unlike steam locomotives, which took hours to warm up ready for action. After the war, more economical diesel versions were developed and began to be used as shunters on the main railway network. The wartime light-rail experiment was in some ways the first nail in the coffin for the steam locomotive, foreshadowing its replacement with the diesel and electric engines we see today.

The utility of the war's Lilliputian light railways endured beyond the end of the fighting. When peace finally arrived, the people of France and Flanders were left surveying the devastation. Whole villages had been

BELOW AND TOP RIGHT Scenes of devastation in the Somme district.

BOTTOM RIGHT An advertisement in the *Railway Gazette* for some of the light-railway equipment used during the war.

destroyed. What had been fertile farmland was unrecognizable, churned into muddy bogs. The task of reconstructing the war-torn landscape was immense, and light rail was used extensively for the job. The lines carried building materials and labour, and also refugees returning to their ravaged homes.

This vital work complete, most of the light railways were dismantled and their tracks and rolling stock sold off. Agriculture and industry were quick to snap up these bargains, and British companies such as Smith's Potato Crisps used former military equipment to build light railways for their businesses. A very few railways remained in place: in the Somme valley, a wartime route was taken over by the sugar-beet industry and still survives today as a heritage line – the P'tit Train de la Haute Somme. In Britain, a number of First World War era locomotives and wagons have been preserved by the Moseley Railway Trust as part of its collection of industrial light-railway equipment, and they can occasionally be seen in action on the Apedale Valley Light Railway in Staffordshire.

FEEDING MORALE – FOOD SUPPLY ON
THE FRONT AND AT HOME

From the ordinary Tommy's point of view, the most important cargo carried by the railways was not bullets but bully-beef. Huddled in dugouts, the British Army wasn't doing much marching, but its stomach was still a pressing concern. By autumn 1918, taking into account servicemen, civilian volunteers and labourers, plus liberated French and Belgian civilians, there were around 2.6 million mouths to feed on the Western Front. For the railways, supplying this hungry horde was a formidable task.

According to Geoff Clarke, who has been researching the logistics of supplying the Western Front, soldiers received a daily allowance

of around 4,100 calories. This included meat, bread, bacon, cheese, vegetables, butter, jam and tea – although in reality 'vegetables' often meant potatoes and onions, 'hard tack' biscuits were substituted for part of the bread ration, and meat frequently came out of a tin. By 1918, the army was issuing an astonishing 67 million pounds of meat and 90 million pounds of bread every month. The railways were the only practical means of transporting this vast bulk, and they soon formed the spine of a sophisticated distribution system.

Most goods arrived first at one of the Channel ports, from where they were taken by rail to marshalling yards known as 'regulating stations'. Here, the port traffic would converge with dedicated trains bringing in items like bread – fresh from the army's immense bakeries – or produce bought locally in France. These supplies were then sorted into mixed trainloads up to fifty wagons long. A single train would contain everything needed by two infantry divisions – by 1918, some 25,000 men – for one day, from soldiers' rations to forage for horses, plus ammunition, coal and equipment for building and repairing trenches, railways and roads.

The French standard-gauge network would carry this haul as far as the railheads, where it would be parcelled out into smaller loads. Light rail or motor transport took the rations as far as divisional dumps, then finally horse and mule transport would deliver the supplies to the battalion quartermasters' stores and the kitchens, immediately behind the front line.

One of the busiest points in this complex web was the so-called Advanced Supply Depot at Abancourt. Today, this sleepy French village,

BELOW A British field kitchen at Amiens.

surrounded by fields and situated halfway between Amiens and Rouen, bears no obvious trace of its wartime history. But at its peak, Abancourt was home to a sprawling complex of warehouses and train tracks – a 'Camp Bastion' of its day.

According to Geoff Clarke, this hive of activity grew up as a response to the changing demands of the war. As the size of the British Expeditionary

LEFT French officers dining in style at the Front. Conditions for the regular French troops were more basic.

Force mushroomed in 1915–16, the ports became increasingly congested. More space was urgently needed for storing and organizing supplies. However, at Le Havre and the inland port of Rouen – the main supply ports for the southern stretch of the British sector – there was no space to grow. So the army logisticians looked inland for a place to establish an intermediate depot. In Abancourt, at the junction of several key rail routes linking the Somme valley with the coast, they found the perfect spot.

By 1916, the complex stretched along two miles of track around the country junction, and during the Somme campaign that year it supplied a peak of 1.3 million troops with their daily rations. At Le Havre and Rouen, ships disgorged their supplies, which were packed into trains and dispatched towards Abancourt. There, they were unloaded into warehouses containing vast stores of non-perishable foods – enough to keep the southern troops of the British sector supplied for at least a month. Working seven days a week, Abancourt's labourers filled an average of twenty-two supply trains every day, ready to send on to the regulating stations.

It made for an awe-inspiring sight. One visitor recorded his first impressions of the bustling complex, reproduced in a themed collection of first-person accounts of the war, *Living on the Western Front: Annals and Stories, 1914–1919*: 'This amazing supply base from which a million troops are fed – mountains of hay, bacon, jam, pickles, oatmeal, flour – Chinese, kaffir and Jamaican native labour, also English. Saw the food specially imported for Chinese – nameless horrors of seaweed, dried cuttle fish.'

The Chinese consumers of these 'nameless horrors' were civilian labourers. In the latter stages of the war, the initially neutral Chinese government permitted British and French representatives to recruit

BELOW British soldiers cooking on the march.

thousands of Chinese men, transporting them usually from rural China to the Western Front. There, in return for little pay, they took no part in the fighting but helped with the backbreaking work of loading supplies at depots like Abancourt, building roads and railways and other physical tasks. And they weren't the only men at the Front with 'exotic' tastes. Serving alongside the homegrown Tommies were thousands of troops from the Colonies and Dominions, and the authorities attempted to provide familiar food to soldiers from India, Africa, the West Indies and elsewhere. Imports flooded into the Western Front from all over the globe – even British basics like meat and cheese often came from as far afield as New Zealand.

British producers did their bit too, and back home military food supplies placed yet another burden on the already overloaded railway system. One of the least-loved items on the menu in the trenches was a tinned meat and vegetable ration known as 'Maconochie stew'. According to *The Long Trail,* a dictionary of trench slang published after the war: 'Warmed in the tin, "Maconochie" was edible; cold, it was a man-killer. By some soldiers it was regarded as a welcome change from bully-beef.'

This dubious pleasure was manufactured by Maconochie Brothers in Lowestoft in Suffolk, who churned out 40,000 tons a year. The job

ABOVE A Chinese labour battalion assembling track.

RIGHT An Indian soldier cooking in France.

of transporting it to the UK ports fell in the first instance to the Great Eastern Railway, who also had to manage a further 20,000 tons produced by Maconochies' rivals Mortons. Meanwhile, for the London and North Western Railway it was fresh meat supplies that provided the headache. They were given responsibility for organizing the 'military meat traffic', which meant procuring some 22,000 refrigerated railway vans in the space of just nine months.

In addition to the troops' regular requirements, the railways were frequently called upon to transport edible special deliveries. For example, according to Edwin Pratt's 1921 survey of the railways' role in the war, in 1917 British trains helped provide a much-needed festive morale boost:

> . . . the Railway Executive Committee consented to convey free of charge for the British and Foreign Sailors' Society, Sailors' Palace, Commercial Road . . . 20,000 portions of Christmas pudding which that Society desired to forward to the Senior Naval Officers at various naval bases for distribution among the men serving there on trawlers and drifters.

Similar 'comforts' were distributed at Christmases throughout the war, and the railways also delivered an unusual source of nourishment and succour to those who had been invalided off the battlefield. The National Egg Collection for the Wounded, organized by the War Office, encouraged the civilian population to donate freshly laid eggs to speed the recovery of injured soldiers. Across the country, patriots of all ages collected the eggs, then ordinary passenger services carried them for free to one of the designated depots, where they were sorted and forwarded on to military hospitals. At the peak of the scheme, 1.4 million eggs a week were being collected. Sometimes, the names and addresses of the donors were written on the eggs, and the soldiers were able to write thank-you letters, like this one sent by a Wiltshire soldier and reproduced in *Philanthropy and Voluntary Action in the First World War*:

> In the battle of . . . I had the misfortune to be shot through the head; I was taken to hospital, and after being made comfortable in bed my first meal consisted of an egg bearing your address, and as I come from Wootton Bassett I thought I must write and thank

you for it. I wish you could see the joy on the poor fellows' faces when they get the eggs; it would fully repay you for all your trouble. Again thanking you, Yours truly, T. Tucker.

Of course, it wasn't just servicemen who needed to be fed in wartime. On the home front, the railways had to keep normal civilian food supplies flowing, and there was constant tension between this vital work and the demands placed on the network by military traffic. The Ministry of Munitions even lobbied for the definition of 'essential foodstuffs' to be narrowed – ensuring such fripperies as beer, wines and sweets would not be given precedence on the tracks over materials needed for munitions.

As the conflict dragged on, food shortages on the home front became an increasingly pressing issue. From 1917 onwards, the situation was especially dire, as the German campaign of unrestricted submarine warfare began to bite. As ships laden with precious imported food were sent to the bottom of the sea, Britain urgently needed to cut its reliance on imports, and the authorities called on citizens to do their bit by growing their own food.

Keen to help, the railway companies realized they had a valuable resource at their disposal. All along the thousands of miles of tracks running up and down the country lay little strips and parcels of land, much of it unused. Some was already leased to employees as allotments, but the new crisis spurred a major expansion of the scheme. The companies offered plots at little or no rent, and staff leapt at the chance to provide extra food for their families.

Soon, travellers throughout the land could spy these railway gardens from their train windows. Plots were carved out of the most unpromising urban spaces – employees of the London and South Western Railway based at Nine Elms went as far as digging up an old locomotive yard to turn it into a vegetable garden, and there were allotments next to the company's power station at Wimbledon. The management of the London and South Western even organized produce competitions for the staff, with handsome prizes for the best fruit and vegetables.

These horticultural adventures were just one way in which the industry showed solidarity with the war effort. Across the country, railway workers were doing their bit. Railway musical societies entertained the troops. First aiders volunteered at hospitals in their spare time. Staff of the Great Eastern Railway even founded a Knitting Association, buying and sending out wool to knitters across the network, who produced warming scarves and socks for company men serving abroad. But one worker on the Great Western Railway chose to express his patriotism not in actions, but in words. For the railways had their very own war poet.

THE BATH RAILWAY POET

The First World War sparked a literary outpouring that continues to shape our view of the conflict. From the trenches, poetry emerged which evokes both the horror and the fortitude of the battlefield. It conjures images more vivid and haunting than anything captured by a grainy newsreel or photograph, and the works of Siegfried Sassoon, Wilfred Owen, Robert Graves and Rupert Brooke are still studied by schoolchildren today. However, not every wartime writer enjoyed such enduring fame. For a brief moment during the war, Henry Chappell, a.k.a. the Bath Railway Poet, was an international celebrity, but his story has since been forgotten.

Henry Chappell was born in London in 1874 and joined the Great Western Railway in 1891. By the eve of the war he was working in Bath as a porter, where, inspired by the railways and the wide range of human life he saw on the platform, he enjoyed a hobby writing poetry. Indeed, his earliest published poem commemorated the first-ever non-stop journey from London to Plymouth in 1903, by a train carrying the Prince and Princess of Wales.

When war came, ill-health prevented Chappell from signing up. But he quickly found an alternative outlet for his patriotic fervour. Chappell penned a stridently anti-German poem, 'The Day', and sent it off to the newspapers. It was printed in the *Daily Express* on 22 August 1914 and became an overnight sensation.

The poem is written as a warning to Germany that it will rue 'the Day' it plunged the continent into war. Chappell pins the blame for the conflict firmly on Germany: '*You dreamed for the Day, you schemed for the Day*', and paints a picture of the enemy as callous, heartless monsters. He describes the Germans as '*Blasphemer, braggart and coward all*', '*steeped in blood as a hog in slime*', and threatens that '*Not all the waters of all the Rhine / Can wash thy foul hands clean*'.

To the modern reader, the violence of this anti-German language is quite shocking. But in the febrile atmosphere of summer 1914 Chappell's poem struck a chord. As the first waves of British troops were boarding trains for Belgium, the papers were alive with stories of German atrocities. Accounts of the killing and rape of Belgian civilians proliferated and encouraged more young men to join the queues of volunteers lining up outside recruiting offices. This anti-German feeling pre-dated the outbreak of war – indeed, in the early 1900s, spy scares had people suspecting the worst of every German waiter and tourist, a sentiment 'The Day' reflects in the line *'You spied for the Day, you lied for the Day'*.

Emotions were running high, and 'The Day' expressed them perfectly. The poem was soon being displayed in newsagents' windows up and down the country, but that wasn't the limit of its reach. In 1918, an article appeared in the *New York Times*, written by an American who had been in Britain in summer 1914 and seen the popularity of the poem:

> *. . . when I returned to America, it had got there before me: it was in New York, printed on a kind of lavish Christmas card. It was in the Rocky Mountains. From the Atlantic to the Pacific it was quoted and made the subject of articles. While trained literary men were selecting phrases, a railway porter had expressed the indignation of two continents.*

Henry Chappell attracted the attention of big names in the literary world. Rudyard Kipling is said to have complimented him on his work and even travelled to Bath to visit him. In 1918, a collection entitled *The Day and Other Poems* was published and graced with an introduction by Sir Herbert Warren, President of Magdalen College, Oxford, and a former professor of poetry. Sir Herbert recollects the moment he first came across 'The Day' in a stationer's window in Oxford, and praises its author:

> *Mr Chappell is, as he ought to be, a 'poet of the people' . . . His poems are the outcome of his own life. Is it fanciful to say that he has the rhythmic resonance of a locomotive at full speed . . . what he himself so aptly calls 'the cheerful clank of the gleaming crank'?*

The Day.

By HENRY CHAPPELL.

[The author of this magnificent poem is Mr. Henry Chappell, a railway porter at Bath. Mr. Chappell is known to his comrades as the "Bath Railway Poet." A poem such as this lifts him to the rank of a national poet.]

You boasted the Day, and you toasted the Day,
    And now the Day has come.
Blasphemer, braggart and coward all,
Little you reck of the numbing ball,
The blasting shell, or the "white arm's" fall,
    As they speed poor humans home.

You spied for the Day, you lied for the Day,
    And woke the Day's red spleen.
Monster, who asked God's aid Divine,
Then strewed His seas with the ghastly mine;
Not all the waters of all the Rhine
    Can wash thy foul hands clean.

You dreamed for the Day, you schemed for the Day;
    Watch how the Day will go.
Slayer of age and youth and prime
(Defenceless slain for never a crime)
Thou art steeped in blood as a hog in slime,
    False friend and cowardly foe.

You have sown for the Day, you have grown for the Day;
    Yours is the Harvest red.
Can you hear the groans and the awful cries?
Can you see the heap of slain that lies,
And sightless turned to the flame-split skies
    The glassy eyes of the dead?

You have wronged for the Day, you have longed for the Day
    That lit the awful flame.
'Tis nothing to you that hill and plain
Yield sheaves of dead men amid the grain;
That widows mourn for their loved ones slain,
    And mothers curse thy name.

But after the Day there's a price to pay
    For the sleepers under the sod,
And Him you have mocked for many a day—
Listen, and hear what He has to say:
"Vengeance is mine, I will repay."
    What can you say to God?

Reprinted from the London "Daily Express" (Copyright).

Sincerely Yours
Henry Chappell

The slim volume from 1918 contains more poems inspired by the war. In a similar vein to 'The Day', 'His Crown of Shame' rebukes Germany for the sinking of the *Lusitania*, the passenger liner torpedoed by a German U-boat off the coast of Ireland in 1915 with the loss of over a thousand lives. Among the passengers were civilians from neutral America, including high-profile figures such as the millionaire Alfred Vanderbilt. The incident caused an international outcry, and Chappell claims that *'no devil's spawn conceived a fouler crime'*.

There are verses celebrating the contribution of troops from the British Dominions. 'The Rose and the Maple Leaf', for example, paints a picture of Britain and Canada united as part of *'An Empire knit in one vast Brotherhood'*, while 'The Anzacs' praises the *'young blood'* of the Australians and New Zealanders who came *'to fight for a land they only knew / From a mother's lips, or sire's'*. There's even a hymn to Lord Kitchener, offering him *'all good wishes from a humble scribe'*.

Despite being a published poet, Chappell never gave up his railway career. Indeed, the author of the *New York Times* article describes how on the very day the book came out, Chappell could be found going about his ordinary duties at Bath and reveals that apparently he donated the whole of his hundred-pound fee to the Red Cross.

Chappell died in 1937 and his wartime fame was soon all but forgotten. In the post-war era, perspectives on the war changed, and patriotic pride was replaced by an emphasis on the human tragedy of the war and a more critical view of the actions of Britain's military and political leaders. By the later twentieth century, Chappell's vehemently partisan line would have seemed unfashionable, even uncomfortable. Yet his best-selling poem bears witness to the public mood in August 1914. From the vantage point of his platform at Bath, this railway porter watched the British people's reaction to the outbreak of war and captured it in a way that resonated across the land.

STATION CANTEENS

For the four long years of the war, Britain's railways teemed with men in uniform. Troop trains packed with new recruits headed to the Front – crossing paths with the travelling ambulances that brought home their wounded comrades. Leave brought precious respite from the fighting, but before the longed-for reunion with family and friends there were tedious railway journeys to endure. With the network under unprecedented pressure, delays were common and carriages crowded. Battle-weary men often arrived in stations at odd hours of the day and night, only to face a long and uncomfortable wait for their connecting train.

Compared to the hardships of the trenches, these inconveniences must have paled into insignificance. But for the civilian population, the battlefield was far off and out of sight, while the trains full of suffering soldiers were a visible reminder of the servicemen's sacrifice. They soon sparked a grass-roots movement that saw volunteers handing out free refreshments to troops at railway stations up and down the land.

Pratt suggests that the movement started at Perth in Scotland, where a group of enterprising ladies took it upon themselves to start offering fruit, tea and cake to soldiers passing through. Before long, this ad-hoc arrangement had mutated into a serious catering operation, staffed from 5 a.m. through to 1 a.m. the next day. Meanwhile, south of the border, similar ideas were germinating. According to Sandra Gittins, who has written a history of the Great Western Railway in the war, a Red Cross volunteer in Banbury, Oxfordshire, was distressed to read that thirsty soldiers had resorted to drinking the water from the station fire buckets. Like the ladies in Perth, she resolved to do something about it and began offering lemonade to the trainloads of troops.

The idea spread like wildfire. Public donations flooded in, allowing volunteers to set up all kinds of arrangements. In York, the North Eastern Railway provided a pair of old carriages that were used to set up a buffet. In Exeter, local ladies put together packed lunches containing sandwiches, fruit, cake and cigarettes, which they distributed from the platform. Many of the volunteers were also Red Cross nurses, and some stations were designated rest stations for ambulance trains. Alongside food and drink, some stations made it easy for patients to stay in touch with loved ones, offering postcards pre-printed with a basic message such as: 'I am passing through this station in an Ambulance Train on my way to Hospital at . . . I will write again as soon as I get settled down in Hospital.'

Perhaps the most impressive refreshments operations were those offered in London's major termini, where free buffets were established to serve the huge numbers of troops passing through the capital en route to and from the various theatres of war. Victoria station was one of the busiest, bringing in troops on the South Eastern and Chatham line from Folkestone, the main port through which troops passed on their way to and from the Western Front. But it was a little tardy in providing them with comforts.

In February 1915, Victoria came in for some criticism in the form of an anonymous letter to *The Times*:

It is rather unpleasant to arrive here, returning on leave . . . to find all doors closed. At Boulogne the Red Cross Association has a room in the station always open and with a huge supply of tea and coffee for troops passing through. Surely London can do something of the same sort.

RIGHT The Soldiers' Free Buffet at Charing Cross station. Similar canteens were set up at railway termini across London, providing refreshments to soldiers passing through.

Signed 'Cold' and 'On Leave', the letter encouraged the speedy opening of an all-day free buffet. Victoria's operation became the biggest of all the London station buffets, serving between 3,000 and 4,000 men a day and getting through almost 3,000 lb of cake and 1,700 loaves a week.

By the end of the war, the railway stations had come to represent a beacon of warmth for hungry, cold, exhausted troops. The railways on the home front were feeling the pinch, but in this small way they could try to alleviate the servicemen's pain. Even after the war was over, the success of the 'Free Buffet' movement was a source of pride, as shines through in railway historian Edwin Pratt's 1921 assessment:

Well supported by the British public, it conferred incalculable benefits on untold millions of men; it diminished the strain of their long journeys; it showed them the genuine sympathy of those on whose behalf they were fighting, and it helped them to retain their fighting strength and to return to their duties overseas in better spirits and in greater vigour than, humanly speaking, would otherwise have been possible.

QUINTINSHILL – THE WORST RAILWAY DISASTER IN BRITISH HISTORY

In another expression of Britain's fighting spirit, 'business as usual' was the official slogan in the early days of the war. British industry would not be cowed, and that included the all-powerful railway companies. They were determined to maintain usual service, despite the added strains of troop traffic and munitions transport. Unfettered railway expansion in Victorian times had left Britain with plenty of spare capacity, and, amazingly, after the initial disruption of mobilization, near-normal timetables were quickly resumed. For ordinary Britons, this must have been a source of reassurance at a troubling time. War had turned everything upside down, but you could still rely on the rails to get you where you needed to go. However, this confidence was about to be badly shaken. For the war years witnessed one of railway history's blackest hours – a catastrophic multi-train smash that remains unmatched in scale to this day.

In the early hours of 22 May 1915, at Larbert in Stirlingshire, the 7th Battalion, Royal Scots were boarding troop trains. The men were territorials from Leith and had been working on home defence since the start of the conflict. But now they were about to join the fighting abroad. They would travel by rail to Liverpool, where they were scheduled to board the troopship *Aquitania* and set sail for the Mediterranean. There, at Gallipoli on the western coast of modern-day Turkey, the Mediterranean Expeditionary Force was fighting the troops of Germany's ally the Ottoman Empire. The land battle had got off to a dismal start, and the men of the 7th Royal Scots were being sent as much-needed reinforcements.

To move the 1,028 men and their kit, three trains were required. The troops would travel in the first two, with the third, containing the horses and other vital equipment, following behind. With rolling stock hard to come by, the trains were made up from a rag-bag assortment of coaches that had been cobbled together from different companies. Roughing it was part and parcel of wartime transport, and the men were crammed into old-fashioned wooden-framed carriages, lit by gas stored in cylinders beneath the floor. According to J. A. B. Hamilton's 1969 account, the first train departed at around 3.30 a.m. As it chugged through the Scottish countryside, many of the servicemen on board would have grabbed the chance to catch up on sleep as best they could in the uncomfortable wagons.

By around half past six, the train was nearing the English border. Just north of Gretna was an isolated signal box, known as Quintinshill, and as the troop train approached, it was speeding along at around seventy miles per hour, despite the antiquated coaches. But then the driver rounded a bend to reveal a terrifying sight. There, right in his path, was a stationary passenger train. He slammed on the brakes, but it was too late.

The driver and fireman were almost certainly killed instantly as their locomotive ploughed into the parked train at around forty miles per hour. The force of the impact sent coaches flying through the air – some went right over the top of the tender, while others were thrown onto the opposite track. Many of the soldiers must have been injured and some were probably killed by this initial impact. But the number of casualties will never be known, because just a minute later, as men attempted to

scramble out of the overturned wagons, from the opposite direction an express train from London came flying up the track.

The express smashed into the debris from the first crash – and into the escaping soldiers. More wreckage was scattered, this time damaging a goods train and a coal train waiting in passing loops beside the line. Now, the collision became a catastrophe: hot coals from the engines had sparked a fire. Fuelled by the gas canisters, the wooden carriages were quickly engulfed by the inferno.

Many soldiers were trapped in the carriages, and witnesses later described their cries as the fire blazed. There are even stories of officers firing their weapons through carriage windows to put an end to the men's agony. It took hours to quell the flames, and by the end of the day the death toll stood at an estimated 230, with 246 injured. Among the dead

ABOVE Fire and smoke pour from one of the sleeping cars of the express train at Quintinshill.

RIGHT The victims of the disaster being treated next to the track.

were twelve passengers from the express train – several of them officers on leave, making their way home to Scotland – and a mother and baby from the local service. But the troop train had fared the worst. Of the fatalities, 214 were men of the 7th Royal Scots. Of the 485 officers and men who had left Larbert that morning, fewer than 70 uninjured survivors gathered together at four o'clock that afternoon.

The Quintinshill disaster remains the worst railway accident in British history. Shockingly, this multiple tragedy had unfolded due to human error. The signalman on duty had given the troop train the green light to advance – despite the passenger train already on the track.

The backstory to this moment was a catalogue of mistakes and misdemeanours. Amazingly, James Tinsley, the signalman who waved the troop train through, had himself alighted from the ill-fated passenger train just minutes earlier. Against regulations, he had used it to

travel to the signal box where he was due to take over from the night signalman, George Meakin. In fact, by prearrangement with Meakin – but without official permission – he was running half an hour late.

As Tinsley arrived, Meakin was deciding how to handle an upcoming influx of trains. On a busy route from London to Scotland via Carlisle, Quintinshill was something of a hotspot for congestion, and alongside the track were two passing loops where slow trains could be shunted to allow faster ones through. On 22 May, Meakin's problem was the northbound stopping service on which Tinsley had hitched a ride. It was blocking the path of two expresses from London that were due to pass shortly, but the loops were already occupied. On one side was a goods train, on the other an empty coal train, returning from having refuelled the fleet at Scapa Flow. So Meakin decided to shunt the local service over onto the 'wrong' track, to wait for the two express trains to pass before continuing its journey. The signals would protect it, making sure no other trains came through. It should have been perfectly safe.

With that, he handed over the reins to Tinsley, who proceeded to fill in the last half-hour's records in his own handwriting, to cover up his late arrival. Against all signal-box rules, Meakin hung around, making

LEFT AND ABOVE The scene of devastation at Quintinshill, site of the worst railway disaster in British history.

chit-chat and reading the paper. The first express passed without incident. Then Tinsley made his fatal mistake. It has been suggested that he was too busy concentrating on his record-keeping, or perhaps distracted by the hubbub in the signal box, but however it happened Tinsley completely forgot about the train Meakin had just shunted. This lapse of memory seems inexplicable – this was the very same service he had ridden to work, which with a little effort he could have seen through the window.

Unfortunately, procedures designed to safeguard against such human frailty, such as placing a special collar on the signal lever as a reminder that the line was blocked, hadn't been followed by Meakin. When a request came from the next signal box to send the troop train south along the line, Tinsley accepted it. By the time he and Meakin realized the terrible truth, the first crash was unfolding – and they were also too late to stop the second of the express trains hurtling into the wreckage.

The signalmen's mistakes had devastating consequences. But arguably the war had also played its part. The combustible wooden carriages, with their lethal gas lighting – old fashioned even at the time – were pressed into service owing to the demands of the conflict. Yet the troop-train driver, perhaps under pressure to get the men to Liverpool on time, was making this rickety stock do express-train speeds. War traffic had also brought unusual congestion to the line around Gretna: neither the coal train nor the troop train would ordinarily have been on the tracks. Despite these 'specials', the normal schedule of expresses, freight trains and local services were expected to continue operating. At Quintinshill, 'business as usual' had a tragic outcome.

Meakin and Tinsley were later tried and found guilty of culpable homicide, and both served prison sentences. More recently, Adrian Searle and his co-author Jack Richards have put forward a new interpretation of the story. Their book argues that the signalmen were made scapegoats and that the railway company responsible for the line and the Railway Executive Committee, running the railways on behalf of the government, should have taken far more responsibility for their part in the accident. Their case rests on evidence that suggests Tinsley was suffering from a serious medical condition, possibly epilepsy, and that he was very ill on the day of the crash – a complicating factor the railway authorities didn't want publicly broadcast. They even contend that central government attempted to hush up the incident, arguing that it could ill-afford further denting of the nation's morale when the country was already reeling from the sinking of the *Lusitania* and the poor start to the Gallipoli campaign.

Wherever the blame truly lay, for the 7th Royal Scots the accident was a devastating blow. The small band of survivors from the crash continued on to Liverpool, but only the officers made it to Gallipoli; the rest of the traumatized men were declared unfit for service and sent home instead. The rest of the battalion set sail without them, only to be decimated on the battlefield. By mid July, the Quintinshill disaster and the ill-fated foreign expedition had reduced the battalion's strength from 1,028 to just 174 men. Today, a memorial to the members of the battalion who died on British soil stands at the site of the accident.

The accident prompted some soul-searching by the railway companies, and the various merits of traffic-control systems and fire precautions were debated. But it was not an opportune moment for railway reform. As 1915 wore on, and the prospect of a swift end to the war receded, the effects of conflict began to be felt on the home front. With ever more war work to do, the railways struggled to maintain their pre-war performance. Services were cancelled and stations closed. Travel for pleasure was discouraged, and the term 'joyriding' was coined as a slur on those who persisted in such indulgence.

War was changing the railways. Some of the changes would be difficult, perhaps impossible to reverse. But it would all be worth it – if the rails could help bring the conflict to a close.

CHAPTER 4

ON TRACK TO VICTORY

By the middle years of the First World War, the tentacles of the conflict had reached into every part of British society. This was total war. Military strategy alone could not guarantee victory; both sides had to draw on every possible resource at their disposal.

While the guns blazed on the Western Front, spies worked in secret behind enemy lines to try to gain the edge in the intelligence war. Both sides attempted to starve one another into submission by preventing imports reaching their enemy's civilian populations. Rationing was introduced, to eke out supplies and prevent civilian unrest. Propaganda was produced on an unprecedented scale, in a bid to win the battle for hearts and minds. And alongside the vast armies, civilians were mobilized – growing food, making weapons and taking on the jobs of men sent to fight.

For some in Britain, this upheaval was an unwelcome disruption to the old order, heralding change that might prove difficult to reverse when peace returned. For others, it brought new opportunities to break out of the straitjacket of traditional roles, foreshadowing the profound social transformation that the twentieth century would bring. On the railways, the turmoil of war forced new working practices and the creative exploitation of existing resources. And as the combatants turned to new technologies in their desire to gain the advantage, there was the first hint that the railway age might be drawing to a close.

WOMEN ON THE RAILS

The First World War was a watershed for Britain's railways in many ways, but perhaps the most visible transformation was an influx of female faces – on station concourses and platforms; in ticket offices and locomotive sheds; even in the hallowed sanctum of the signal box. The number of women railway employees jumped from around 13,000 when war broke out to a maximum of almost 69,000 in September 1918. Without them, the railways might have ground to a halt. But for the country's railwaymen, and the British public, it was a change that took some getting used to.

In 1914, although some women were employed by the railway companies, the roles open to them were heavily circumscribed. In her book charting the history of women railway workers, Helena Wojtczak

ABOVE Female railway
workers – they were
kept behind the scenes
before the demands of
war thrust them into
the limelight.

describes how they were found staffing ladies' waiting rooms, doing
clerical work in back offices, sewing upholstery in carriage works and
washing the railways' dirty laundry, among other menial tasks. But
public-facing roles were few and far between, and the more highly paid
skilled jobs were designated 'male grades'. Altogether, women made
up just 2 per cent of the workforce – the Edwardian railway trade was
overwhelmingly a man's world.

But almost as soon as war broke out, male-dominated industries
began to feel the hit. Railwaymen disappeared from their jobs in droves
– just eleven days after war was declared, 27,600 had either enlisted
or been called up to join territorial or reservist units. And even this
wasn't enough to satisfy the trenches' voracious appetite for men. As

the mass recruitment campaign to build the 'New Army' got under way in 1914–15, the War Office began making noises, suggesting that the railways find a way to release more workers for service. The Railway Executive Committee faced a quandary: railwaymen must be allowed to do their duty, yet the extra demands the war placed on the railways meant they could ill-afford to haemorrhage staff. There was only one possible solution. Women workers would have to step into men's shoes.

From spring 1915, women were allowed to apply for some roles previously designated 'men-only'. Railway wages were vastly superior to rates of pay for domestic service and other traditional female occupations, and thousands leapt at the chance to work as ticket collectors, porters, carriage cleaners, even guards on board trains.

As the first of the new recruits appeared in public, the reaction ranged from fascination to horror. Some, such as the writer of an article in the June edition of the *Railway Review*, quoted in Rosa Matheson's *The Fairer Sex*, feared the consequences of exposing fragile ladies to the hurly burly of life on the platform: 'The ticket collector is often exposed to the calumnies of a rough element which passes through the ticket gates and this is the objectionable part of the position, unsuited to the fairer sex.'

The women themselves appear to have taken this danger in their stride. In *Capital Cities at War*, Adrian Gregory cites a *Daily Mail* interview with a new 'ticket collectress', who coolly observed: 'Of course all sorts of men come by train . . . some of them were inclined at first to be facetious and pass remarks, but it does not take them long to get over it.'

But this relaxed attitude wasn't shared by everyone. One would-be fare-dodger on the Great Central Railway tried to use the shock factor of women railway workers to his advantage, according to a report published in the *Coventry Evening Telegraph* in July 1915:

> *Arriving in Manchester from Marple, he gave up, when asked for his ticket, an out-of-date ticket . . . His explanation was . . . on arrival at London Road, Manchester, his attention was taken up by seeing women porters in uniform, and he inadvertently gave up the ticket in question. A fine of 10s was imposed.*

Indeed, it was the women's uniforms that really seem to have captured the public imagination, and newspapers seized the chance to print images of photogenic young women in their fetching outfits. In some cases, their specially provided uniforms needed to carefully balance practicality with propriety. Female guards had to swiftly jump on board trains after giving the all-clear, so floor-skimming skirts were dangerously impractical. The compromise settled on by the Metropolitan Railway was a knee-length skirt, beneath which special knee-length knickers were worn, tucked into boots to guarantee the protection of the guards' modesty.

Even more scandalous was the adoption by some women of men's clothing. According to 1920s railway historian Edwin Pratt, this came about thanks to a group of London railwaywomen who took matters into their own hands. They were employed by the London and South Western Railway as carriage cleaners – one of the most common women's occupations, performed by over 2,000 women by the end of 1916. The job was physically strenuous, especially when it came to cleaning the outside of the carriages, which meant scaling ladders and even perching on the roof. The women of the London and South Western soon realized that skirts were not suitable and set about knocking up makeshift

BELOW The women's uniforms were a particular talking point.

trousers for themselves. The idea soon caught on, and for 'backstage' roles breeches became widespread – though women in public-facing roles never adopted the look.

Women were seen as naturals when it came to cleaning, but in other areas doubt was cast on their abilities. Even in clerical roles, women were often accepted only grudgingly, as recounted by NER clerk May Atkinson, quoted in Wojtczak's *Railwaywomen*:

> *The man who had to train me had held the job for over twenty years and did not take kindly to a girl of twenty taking over, so I didn't have it so good for the first week. But I didn't complain or weep as some girls did. In time he was quite friendly and told me to consult him if I had any difficulties.*

So when it came to the skilled operating grades, such as signalman, it is unsurprising that there was fierce opposition to the idea that men could be replaced. Desperately trying to preserve their territory, railwaymen deployed a whole range of arguments. Some purported to have women's

ABOVE A group of Midland Railway cleaners – '21,500 men joined HM Forces. Women "carry on" as Loco Cleaners'.

RIGHT Women cleaners at Crewe in their scandalous breeches.

best interests at heart, fretting that their 'delicate constitutions' would be damaged by the strain of such work. Others exploited the fear factor – especially strong in the wake of the Quintinshill tragedy – warning that the public would be imperilled should easily distracted, flutter-brained ladies be entrusted with the solemn responsibilities of the signal box.

To a certain extent, the naysayers succeeded in placing limits on women railway workers. Women never penetrated the male bastion of the footplate. It was argued that the training required to qualify as an engine driver or fireman would take too long, never mind women's unsuitability for such physically and mentally demanding work. However, despite strong resistance, women were employed as guards, shunters and indeed signalwomen, eventually winning praise for their work from some.

Nowhere was the railway industry's ambivalence about this influx of women more apparent than in the debate over pay. For the railway companies, the issue was simple – employing women couldn't be avoided, and ideally this new resource should be put to use as cheaply

LEFT The station
mistress at
Broughton Cross.

ABOVE A woman porter
on the platform at
Orpington station.

as possible. But for the unions, representing the overwhelmingly male
workforce, things were trickier. They didn't really want women there
in the first place, arguing that they weren't up to the job. But if they
were to be employed, they mustn't be allowed to undercut hard-won
male pay rates, which could lead to permanent wage decreases for men
or their permanent replacement by cheaper women. Helena Wojtczak
elegantly sums up the paradox: 'the companies argued that women were

Orpington Station.

competent but should be paid less than men; the unions contended that women were not as capable as men, but wanted them to get equal pay'.

The uneasy compromise reached was to pay women in male roles the minimum agreed rate for the job – the same as a temporary male worker would receive. Unlike permanent male staff, women didn't receive an annual pay rise, and to start with were not eligible for the so-called 'war bonus'. This increase was intended to compensate workers for the high cost of living in wartime Britain – by spring 1917, food costs were 95 per cent higher than they had been in 1914. After much campaigning and even industrial action by some angry railwaywomen, they were eventually granted the bonus at a reduced rate – but in the male grades, women's pay never achieved parity with men's, and in traditionally female roles it continued to lag far behind.

By summer 1918, around 65,000 women were working on the railways, some 36,000 of these in male grades. After 1917, when the Bakerloo line was extended to Watford Junction, this new section of the London Underground was run entirely by women, except for the train drivers. It represented an extraordinary social transformation. But this feminization of the rails was not to last. As the war drew to a close and men began returning from the Front, women were asked to vacate their roles to make way for them, under the terms of the 1919 Restoration of Pre-War Practices Act. The railway industry was left with a larger female workforce than before the war, but those women who remained were mostly in back-office positions. The smartly uniformed women who had collected tickets, operated signals and hauled heavy luggage disappeared from view almost as quickly as they had appeared.

It was a microcosm of the return to the old order taking place across the country. By 1921, the percentage of the female population classed as 'gainfully employed' was smaller than it had been in 1911. Although women over thirty were granted the vote in 1918, this was arguably as much down to the pre-war suffragette movement and to a desire to balance out the imagined radicalism of newly enfranchised working-class men as to the impact of war work. For most British women, the end of the fighting was a return to business as usual.

On the railways, women got a second chance to fill men's roles in the Second World War, after which they stayed in greater numbers, but it wasn't until the 1980s that the first woman train driver would take to the tracks.

LONDON LINES

One of the biggest challenges faced by the men and women who ran the railways in wartime was keeping traffic flowing through London. With the main routes to and from the Channel ports all feeding into the capital, and main lines serving manufacturing centres and army bases also terminating there, London became a busy transit point for trains carrying men, munitions and supplies.

But then, as today, the options for crossing the metropolis without changing trains were limited. What few routes there were had sprung up in an unplanned fashion, as part of Britain's organic railway evolution.

Now they were being asked to withstand volumes of traffic that their Victorian builders could not have envisaged. The railways rose to the challenge, wringing every last drop out of the few routes available to them. And a hundred years on, the very same lines that formed this vital wartime network are enjoying a new lease of life as some of the most important arteries in London's twenty-first-century transport system.

For moving troops and supplies from east to west and west to east across the capital, the key line was the North London Railway. Constructed in the mid nineteenth century, the North London Line proper ran from the east London docks to Chalk Farm. There it flowed into the Hampstead Junction and North and South Western Junction Lines, creating a seamless route via Willesden Junction in the north-west of the city all the way through to Kew in the south-west. It had originally been intended as a means of speeding up the transit of goods to and from the Port of London, and all along its route were links to the main lines running in from the industrial centres in the Midlands and the north.

It was soon adopted by city dwellers as a useful passenger route, serving residential destinations across north London. But the outbreak of war meant suburban traffic had to take a back seat, with services disrupted and even suspended. Planners soon realized that from the North London Line, it was possible to transfer directly to the networks of the North Western, Midland, Great Northern and Great Eastern railway companies, and this remarkable array of connections made this fourteen-mile stretch of track invaluable for coordinating the movements of troops and supplies across the capital. In total, more than 13,500 military trains passed over this diminutive line during the course of the war, on top of its usual traffic, with a peak of more than 350 trains in a single two-day period.

Useful as the North London Railway was, it didn't however cross the Thames, the biggest barrier to cross-capital train travel. In 1914, there were just three possible routes for doing so, and all had their role to play in handling the wartime traffic.

Surprisingly, the most direct of these was actually part of the London Underground. In fact, it was a stretch of the capital's very first underground railway line, the Metropolitan route from Paddington to Farringdon Street, which had opened in 1863 and become an overnight success. Indeed, it was so popular that in 1868 extra tracks were added on the busiest stretch between King's Cross and Farringdon, and it was these so-called 'City Widened Lines' that were to become a vital route for war traffic fifty years later.

As railway historian Christian Wolmar explains in his history of the London Underground, the Metropolitan Railway allowed other railway companies to run their trains on its tracks from the start, and these were soon used to create innovative through-routes. From 1866, a tunnel beneath Smithfield market near Farringdon linked the City Widened Lines to the London, Chatham and Dover Railway Company's network, crossing the Thames via a bridge at Blackfriars before joining up south of the river with routes serving south-east England. It made it possible to run direct services through the heart of the capital, and in the late 1800s the train operators experimented with many such routes – for example, a single train from Greenwich in south-east London would take you all the way through to Muswell Hill in the north of the city.

With the coming of war, this direct route linking the north of Britain with the Channel ports was a godsend. Soon, City-bound commuters were vying with military traffic on the tracks. But using these urban lines for the war effort wasn't without its problems. As the City Widened Lines wove a path through the congested cityscape, they had to dip beneath other railway lines, diving underground then rising up again in order to reach the elevated level of the bridge over the Thames. This meant there were steep gradients on the line – no challenge for a lightweight commuter service but a different proposition for heavy wartime coal and munitions trains. At times, two engines had to be used to conquer the slopes, and thanks to this and other troubleshooting by inventive railway workers, almost 250,000 tons of goods were carried on this short stretch of underground during the course of the war.

By the 1960s, the tunnel link beneath Smithfield had fallen out of use. However, it reopened in 1988 as part of the Thameslink route, which connects Brighton with Bedford via central London. Today, this is one of only two direct services through the capital – and the only one to penetrate the city centre – and is currently undergoing a significant expansion programme. The renovated Blackfriars station, with platforms that extend along the length of the bridge itself, is already in operation, and the revamped Thameslink will eventually include a rebuilt London Bridge station, a new rail hub at Farringdon and a new fleet of spacious trains.

The other cross-London route still in operation today is a less well-known service from Croydon to Milton Keynes, which goes via Clapham and Willesden. The core part of this line was also in place when war broke out, and it too played its part in solving the London transport problem. The West London Line, as it was then known, was originally conceived in the heady days of railway mania and proved a flop in its first incarnation. But by 1914 it had been extended and was a useful goods service skirting central London's western flank, with a Thames crossing at Battersea. With the advent of war, it really came into its own, carrying the heavier loads that the City Widened Lines just couldn't handle.

The line fed into Willesden Junction from the south, via an industrial area used for munitions production and other wartime manufactures and the vast railway depot at Old Oak Common. According to Nick Bosanquet, who has hunted down traces of the First World War on the British landscape for his book *Our Land at War*, traffic from the West London route and the North London Line combined to make Willesden Junction one of the busiest spots on the British railway network, Willesden and Old Oak Common between them handling more than 20,000 trains over the course of the conflict.

BELOW Willesden Junction – one of the busiest points on the rail network during the war.

Willesden Junction Station. N.W.

161

The West London route too has recently been given a new lease of life, having been incorporated into the rebranded London Overground network. The Overground brings together into a coherent system various pre-existing routes around London – including the former North London Railway. It has also claimed the third line that crossed the river in wartime London, the remarkable East London Line.

This third and final north–south route through the capital had perhaps the most unusual history of all. It crossed the Thames not via a bridge but a tunnel that used pioneering techniques to burrow beneath the river. The Thames Tunnel opened in 1843 and was originally designed not for trains but for pedestrians. It was the handiwork of Isambard Kingdom Brunel and his father Marc Brunel, and was an extraordinary engineering achievement – but a financial failure. In the 1860s, it was bought by the East London Railway Company, who ran trains through it connecting New Cross with Shoreditch, but it wasn't until the war years that the tunnel really proved its worth. Ambulance trains especially were routed beneath the Thames and on more than one occasion sheltered there during bombing raids on the capital.

ABOVE Michael Portillo travelling on the Overground to Willesden Junction.

RIGHT The Brunels' groundbreaking Thames Tunnel – built between 1825 and 1843 – attracted huge numbers of curious tourists when it first opened.

After the war, the line became part of the London Underground network, but by the start of the twenty-first century was running only a skeleton service and was closed in 2007 in preparation for an ambitious extension plan. In 2010, the East London Line reopened as part of London Overground, and passenger numbers are projected to rise to 40 million a year by 2016, from just 9 million in 2007.

The wartime cross-capital routes have been revived, and soon they will have a new rival in the form of Crossrail, due to open in 2018. It's incredible to think it has taken until now to build an alternative, and that some of the most heavily used lines in twenty-first-century London rely on the same basic infrastructure available to the railway authorities back in 1914. In some ways, the intensive use of these lines in the war years foreshadowed today's railway renaissance in London, which has seen train travel take centre stage in solving the capital's transport problems once again. The railway operators of the First World War already knew what it's taken us a century to re-realize: keeping London moving relies on the railways.

ESPIONAGE – TRAINSPOTTING
WITH A PURPOSE

While British travellers adjusted to disrupted train timetables and the strange sight of women in uniform, behind the German lines the people of north-east France, Belgium and Luxembourg were enduring occupation. Their railways were at the service of the enemy. Local people had experienced terrible violence, and some were used as forced labour for the Germans. Food was scarce, with many reliant on aid parcels sent from America and elsewhere. But the occupied populations were not entirely powerless. Those who dared could turn this uncomfortable proximity to the enemy to their own advantage.

By spying on their occupiers and sharing information with the Allied intelligence services, civilians in occupied countries could make a real difference to the war effort. During the First World War, intelligence-gathering came of age, and the railways were at the heart of the Allies' most successful operations.

For, as German troops travelled by train along the strategic lines of the occupied zone, a hidden army of trainspotters was secretly watching their every move.

The war's first train-watching networks grew up in Belgium. Its railways had been key to the German invasion, and with the establishment of trench warfare they continued to be of paramount importance to the German effort, used intensively to move men and

ABOVE AND LEFT
Propaganda highlighting the fate of the Belgian population under German occupation.

ABOVE Gorman Landsturm troops in Antwerp.

materiel to, from and around the Western Front. If the Allies had prior warning of troop movements through the country, they might be able to predict German attacks and spot potential areas of weakness. But first they needed to recruit their spies.

The invasion had left the Belgian people shocked, fearful, saddened – and angry. During the early months of the war, an estimated 5,500 civilians were killed by German soldiers. Belgian citizens had to stand by and watch while their property and heritage were destroyed, most vividly perhaps in the devastation of the medieval city of Leuven/Louvain, where many buildings, including the ancient library, were burnt to the ground. As the occupation settled down, the extreme violence came to an end, but its legacy was a group of Belgians who were prepared to risk their personal safety in order to resist the invaders.

The train watchers came from all walks of life. There were railway workers and priests; aristocrats and farm labourers; children and septuagenarians. Around a quarter were women, participating more directly in the war than they otherwise could have done. Some railway spies worked for the French and Belgian intelligence services, but the majority were run by British agents, serving various agencies including the military intelligence corps and the forerunner to our modern MI6. Over the course of the war, an astonishing 4,350 Belgians supplied Britain with railway intelligence.

LEFT AND ABOVE
A fifth of the buildings in Leuven/Louvain were destroyed during the German invasion.

Often, the network leaders were given training to help them make sense of the railway movements they observed. They would learn how to tell the difference between a troop train and a munitions supply, and how to identify the different regiments of the German army from uniforms and cap badges. Most importantly, they were instructed on how to recognize a so-called 'constituted unit'. This was a series of up to fifty-two trains, used to transport an entire division of the German army, complete with men, horses, guns and equipment, to a new location. Large-scale troop movements were impossible to hide, sometimes taking days to pass through a particular junction. As the war went on, these constituted units comprised fewer and fewer trains, revealing the diminishing size of German divisions as the fighting took its toll. And, vitally, they provided the Allies with clues when change was afoot behind the German lines.

To make sure no movement was missed, watching the trains was a twenty-four-hour-a-day job. Most railway spies operated from their own

LEFT A German patrol posing behind a warning sign on the death wire.

homes, and whole families often worked in shifts. They developed their own ingenious systems to keep track of what they saw. Some counted the contents of trains using different types of beans to represent horses, soldiers and guns. Others apparently knitted a record, with plain stitch for soldiers and purl for horses.

The most dangerous part of the operation was sharing this carefully gathered information. According to the memoirs of a British military intelligence officer, reproduced in James Morton's book *Spies of the First World War,* the train watchers first put together reports:

'... written through a magnifying glass on very small bits of the thinnest and toughest tissue paper we could procure, by mapping pens in Indian ink, and then rolled into a tiny package which could be secreted almost anywhere about the human body.'

Then, the reports had to make the treacherous trip out of the occupied zone. With borders that had slammed shut after the outbreak of hostilities, this was no easy task. For British communications, almost all intelligence from Belgium was meant to go via neutral Holland. But the border was strictly policed, and from 1915 crossing it got even tougher. From April that year, the Germans built an electric fence along the Dutch border, known as the 'death wire'. The 2,000-volt fence eventually stretched for around 120 miles and in places was up to 9 feet high. Smugglers known as *passeurs* undertook the dangerous task of getting past this lethal barrier, risking the twin perils of detection and electrocution.

Even once messages reached Holland, the danger wasn't over. Before it could be used by Britain, information still had to cross the Channel. On several occasions, messages were intercepted by the Germans, exposing Belgian agents who were subsequently captured and executed. This roundabout route via Holland was often also very slow. The length of time it took for train observations to reach their final destination was variable, but it frequently took around three weeks, by which time the information might have lost its value.

By the end of the war, a source of more up-to-date railway information had opened up thanks to a daring British train-watching operation established in occupied Luxembourg. The tale is vividly recounted by Janet Morgan in *The Secrets of Rue St Roch*, a true story that reads like a Hollywood movie script. Under the leadership of Captain (later Major) George Bruce, a British military intelligence officer based in Paris, British agents recruited a well-to-do Luxembourg housewife, Madame Rischard, who was in the French capital visiting her son. Her husband was a doctor who just so happened to be the medical advisor to the Luxembourg railways, and Madame Rischard was persuaded to return home and, with his help, attempt to set up a spy ring from scratch. In an extraordinary example of derring-do, a Belgian officer seconded to British military intelligence flew undetected into Luxembourg in an unpowered hydrogen balloon in order to provide support for the operation.

Not only did Madame Rischard succeed in establishing a train-watching operation but, thanks to an audacious ploy, the intelligence

36655   FIELD TELEPHONE MAN, GERMANY

LEFT AND RIGHT
Twentieth-century war
took advantage of all
available technology.
The Germans had
access to telephone
communications during
the war but lacked the
extensive espionage
network used by
the Allies.

gathered by her agents was able to reach the Allies at record speeds. Amazingly, carefully coded messages detailing train movements were transmitted in plain sight – printed as articles in the pages of a local newspaper, *Der Landwirt*. Unlike messages sent by post, which were subject to the whims of the censors and could be delayed for weeks, newspapers were reviewed and approved rapidly, so copies of *Der Landwirt* could quickly reach subscribers in neutral Switzerland, from

where they were forwarded on to British agents in Paris. This simple but risky scheme succeeded in hugely speeding up communication between train watchers and military intelligence, cutting the transmission time down to around five days.

By the last months of the war, Britain was controlling a train-watching network of extraordinary reach. All the most important railway junctions were covered, and by the time of the armistice the British military leadership could pinpoint all but two German divisions on the Western Front. The information provided by the railway spies was just part of the bigger intelligence picture, with information feeding in from other sources such as battlefield interrogation, aerial reconnaissance and intercepted radio or telephone messages. But while the Germans also used all these other methods, they had no equivalent to the Allied train-watching network.

Some of these railway spies paid a heavy price. According to espionage historian Emmanuel Debruyne, more than 2,000 spies (some train watchers, some in other intelligence roles) were imprisoned during the war. More than 200 were executed, and dozens of others died at the Dutch–Belgian border or in jail. But their efforts weren't in vain. They helped the Allies win the intelligence war – not enough in itself to guarantee overall victory but an important part of the shifting balance of power.

1918 – ON TRACK TO VICTORY

In the early months of 1918, the railway spies began to notice some unusual train movements behind German lines. Men and supplies were moving west. It seemed the Germans were preparing for a major attack. Little did the observers realize but, after three and a half years, the Great War on the Western Front was about to burst out of the trenches. Analysis by First World War expert David Stevenson, who has charted the bloody final months of the fighting in his book *With Our Backs to the Wall*, reveals that the railways played a crucial role.

For most of 1917, Germany had been fighting a defensive war, successfully fending off a series of Allied attacks. But as 1918 dawned, it was time for a change of strategy. Thanks in part to the British naval blockade, the German civilian population had been hit by severe shortages of food and other essentials. The troops too were suffering due to a lack of supplies. It wasn't clear how much longer trench warfare could be sustained. Furthermore, German submarine attacks against American shipping had finally pushed the United States into joining the conflict. So far, only limited numbers of US troops had reached the battlefield, but it was only a matter of time before they arrived in force, to breathe new life into the Allied effort.

In the minds of the German military chiefs, if Germany was to stand a chance of victory on the Western Front, it was now or never. Erich Ludendorff, the Imperial Army's chief strategic planner, masterminded the development of an offensive campaign more ambitious than anyone had yet attempted. In spring 1918, he would unleash an overwhelming attack – codenamed 'Michael' – against what he considered the weakest link in the Allied front line, the British Expeditionary Force. If necessary, this would be followed up by a series of further aggressive assaults. German troops would win a swift victory or die in the attempt.

All the resources of the Reich were thrown behind the plan. In the aftermath of the 1917 Russian Revolution, Germany had negotiated a truce with the Russians, freeing up some half a million men from the Eastern Front. The Germans also removed troops from Italy, where they had been supporting Austro-Hungarian forces, in order to bolster their manpower on the Western Front. In the early months of 1918, the railways

RIGHT General Erich Ludendorff (right), the German army's chief strategic planner, with Chief of the General Staff General Paul von Hindenburg.

thronged with troop trains as men were redeployed in preparation for 'Michael' – according to Stevenson, in the five weeks leading up to the offensive more than 10,000 trains pulled into the attack zone.

The attack would strike along a fifty-mile stretch of the Front in the Somme sector. Behind the German lines, vast amounts of supplies were secretly gathered. As many as 25,000 tons arrived in the area each day, with train movements taking place under cover of darkness to preserve secrecy. By the eve of the battle, the railways had brought in more than 6,500 guns – half the total owned by the German army – and more than a million men were ready to pounce.

Although Allied intelligence had predicted a German offensive, French and British forces didn't know precisely when or where the

assault would come. They also underestimated the scale of the onslaught. They were to be awed by its epic ambition. When 'Michael' began on 21 March 1918, the British defenders were swept before it. German guns fired 3.2 million rounds on the first day alone. Under cover of fog, German infantry took British troops by surprise, and by the end of the day had made average advances of between two and three miles – an achievement unmatched since trench warfare had begun.

But despite this dazzling initial success, the offensive soon ran into trouble. Brimming with confidence, Ludendorff broadened his battle aims, sending troops to fight the French as well as the British, and diluting the main thrust of the attack. What was more, the speed of the advance started to work against the troops. Just as in 1914, the soldiers were soon far ahead of their railheads, and it became increasingly difficult to keep them supplied. Light railways could be built rapidly, but not rapidly enough to keep up with 'Michael'. Horses and lorries were desperately needed, but for the Germans these were in short supply. Thanks to the blockade, stocks of feed for horses as well as petrol for road vehicles – even rubber for tyres – were all running dangerously low.

By early April, the advance had faltered. 'Michael' had not delivered the knockout blow needed to put Britain out of action. Nevertheless, significant gains had been made. The Germans had occupied 1,200 square miles of territory and were within 10 miles of Amiens, a key railway junction for the Allies.

For the British, losing Amiens would dangerously restrict their capacity to supply the southern sector of the Front and to transfer troops between north and south. As soon as they realized the city was threatened, Britain and France cooperated to move in reinforcements by rail. They succeeded in holding the Germans at arm's length, but the enemy was still close enough to shell the line, and the Allies were rattled.

The following months did little to allay their fears. As spring moved into summer, German forces continued their attempt to overwhelm the Allies in a series of further daring attacks up and down the Front, with some spectacular successes. After an assault in Flanders on 9 April, with the vital Hazebrouck railway junction soon under threat and British morale flagging, General Haig issued a rallying cry: 'With our backs to the wall and believing in the justice of our case each one of us must fight on to the end. The safety of our homes and the freedom of mankind alike depend upon the conduct of each one of us at this critical moment.'

Britain felt itself in great danger, but beneath the surface the German effort was beginning to crumble. While trains packed with munitions continued to rumble along the key German rail routes, beyond the railheads supply difficulties bedevilled the campaign. When the underfed German troops came across abandoned Allied stores in newly gained territory they seized on the bounty they found, and the contrast with their own meagre supplies dangerously damaged morale.

The Allied rail network was holding up – but only just. Two years

BELOW The ruins of Amiens in 1919.

had now passed since Sir Eric Geddes's reinvigoration of the French transport infrastructure, and the intervening months had been hard on the railways. The French system was creaking once again. 'Michael' had stretched it further, demanding intensive working of the lines as troops were hastily moved to meet the German threat. Although the Allies had succeeded in defending almost all of their main railway junctions, a German advance in Champagne during May managed to sever a trunk line leading from Paris to the east. And now the French network had a new pressure to contend with. The much-anticipated influx of Americans had finally begun. By March 1918, there were 220,000 US troops in France. During the spring and summer, hundreds of thousands more were shipped over. They brought with them their own railway supplies and operatives, but it wasn't enough to compensate for the extra burden. Indeed, their imported locomotives sometimes caused more problems than they solved – too heavy for the French tracks, they created yet more damage to be repaired.

Still, thanks in part to American support, July 1918 brought a shift in the balance of power. At the Second Battle of the Marne, French forces

BELOW Nineteenth-century technology helps usher in a twentieth-century weapon. An early tank is loaded on a railway wagon ready for transport.

ABOVE Michael Portillo
in the Citadelle de
Montreuil-sur-Mer
with historian David
Stevenson. The town
itself played host to
British Army GHQ,
the nerve centre of
the British logistical
operation.

– fighting alongside American troops and aided by tanks transported by specially built trains – not only checked the Germans but also counter-attacked, for the first time since March, and liberated the trunk line they had lost. This success was closely followed by a British-led attack at the Battle of Amiens, which began on 8 August, forcing the German front line back away from that key railway artery.

The tide had turned, and the Allies seized the initiative. Putting the railway network through its paces once again, they launched a series of offensives dotted all the way up and down the front line, without giving the Germans pause for breath. While Germany struggled to transport troops quickly enough to respond to these scattered attacks, the grid of tracks connecting the different sectors of the Allied front helped carry men and supplies to several different areas in quick succession. In late September, the Allies temporarily paralysed Germany's reinforcement system by launching a synchronized advance.

And by now the Allies also had another weapon in their transport armoury. Alongside the railways, they were increasingly taking advantage of motor vehicles. Unlike Germany, France had invested heavily in automotive technology and by 1918 had a fleet of 37,000 lorries to call on. On 15 July, 120,000 men and 7,000 tons of munitions were driven to the battlefield in a single day. In some ways this was a sign of things to come. By the advent of the Second World War, military logistics would depend on the integration of railway networks with modern road transport. For the civilian railways it was also a portent of change. At the end of the war, the market would be flooded with army-surplus vehicles, many of which were bought by demobbed soldiers who set up transport businesses – a small factor in the railways' decline in the post-war era.

In the heat of battle in 1918, this logistical flexibility helped give the Allies the edge. The Germans – their morale weakened by the collapse of the dreamed-of breakthrough and by ever-greater shortages of food and supplies – buckled under the Allied onslaught. By late September, the Allies had regained all their key railway routes. They then began a steady advance into German-held territory, with the German-run railways in their sights. As they progressed, they captured more and more of the German network, until, in November, a fatally weakened Germany was forced to agree to a ceasefire.

By this stage, the Allies too were rapidly outrunning their railheads. Coupled with the fact that the retreating German troops had destroyed the tracks in their wake, they were beginning to experience supply problems like those that had earlier plagued the Germans. When the armistice came, they were just about still managing to feed and supply the troops, but how much longer they could have sustained this is difficult to say. For the Allies' railways, the ceasefire negotiations came not a moment too soon.

LEFT A railway line cut by shell damage stops an engine in its tracks. As the Germans retreated they also deliberately sabotaged the railways to try to stall the Allied advance.

SUPPLYING THE FLEET

Fighting in the trenches wasn't the only drain on Britain's railway resources. The First World War was also being waged at sea, and for much of the conflict the Grand Fleet was stationed at Scapa Flow off the north coast of Scotland, beyond the reach of the German High Seas Fleet. To supply the fleet in this remote location, lines passing through the barren landscape of the Highlands became some of the most intensively used of the war. For tracks originally built to carry fish and summer tourists, it was a tall order.

There was only one major clash between the Royal Navy and the German High Seas Fleet at the inconclusive Battle of Jutland in 1916. Instead, the war at sea took the form of a battle for trade, with each side trying to throttle the other's supply routes. The aim was to disrupt the war effort and also to starve the civilian populations, undermining support for the war.

The British were the first to implement a naval blockade, and the Grand Fleet's efforts were highly effective. Mines were laid on strategic naval and trade routes. And from their base in the Orkney Islands, menacing warships patrolled the North Sea, scaring neutral vessels away from German ports. In response, the German naval effort went underwater. Submarines known as 'U-boats' made increasingly indiscriminate attacks on Allied shipping. By 1917, the Allies were suffering severe losses, with 869,000 tons of shipping sunk in April alone. But the Allies found a way to protect themselves. Under the convoy system, groups of merchant vessels travelled together under military escort, and this strategy was so successful that by 1918 U-boats were rarely sinking more than 300,000 tons a month.

To help the Royal Navy carry out its mission, it relied on the railways to bring men, munitions, shipbuilding supplies and, above all, coal. The majority of the fleet was coal-powered and depended on supplies from South Wales. Transportation by sea was too risky, so an extraordinary railway operation was begun. Special coal trains, named 'Jellicoe Specials' in honour of the Royal Navy's Commander-in-Chief, were given priority on the network. By 1918, the railways were carrying fifteen Jellicoe specials a day, seven days a week, and it is estimated that some

5.5 million tons of coal were hauled northwards over the course of the war. From Pontypool, this essential cargo had to be carried all the way to Grangemouth on the Firth of Forth, where it was transferred to ships for distribution throughout the fleet – a trip of some 375 miles.

To facilitate the transport of sailors to and from their far-flung bases, a special Naval Service was established in 1917, representing the longest-distance regular service in British railway history. Each day it travelled from London Euston to Thurso station, the terminus of the remote Highland Line, just west of John O'Groats – an epic 717 miles. Understandably, this twenty-two-hour train journey wasn't relished by the ratings, who apparently nicknamed the service the 'misery special'.

Especially in winter, conditions could be difficult – as Edwin Pratt poetically puts it:

> . . . the Highland line traverses the most mountainous, the most rugged, and, in parts, the bleakest and most desolate region in Great Britain – a region where the climate in winter is often extremely rigorous – it is exposed, and especially so in the Far North, to snowstorms, blizzards and floods of a kind and a frequency not equalled on any other railway in the British Isles.

And it wasn't just the passengers who suffered. The single-tracked Highland Line was ill-prepared for transporting all the men and supplies required for a twentieth-century war of the seas, and the conflict almost brought it to its knees. The railway passed through a sparsely populated region and was usually only busy in the summer tourist season. Suddenly, the line had to cope with year-round demands and vastly increased volumes: in 1913 it had carried 2.2 million passengers and 650,000 tons of goods; by 1916 the burden had risen to 4.5 million people and 1.1 million tons.

In 1915, the railway hit a crisis point. Of the 152 locomotives owned by the railway, 50 were so badly broken down that they had been withdrawn, and another 50 were barely managing to limp along, while a chronic shortage of wagons was also causing problems. The rest of the British railway industry was called upon to come to the Highland Line's aid, and somehow reinforcements were found to bolster the line's rolling-stock resources, as companies lent locomotives and engineers.

Against the odds, the tiny line coped with the epic task of supplying the fleet, allowing the Royal Navy to continue its work untroubled by problems of supply. And according to Pratt, the Highland Line's part in this achievement earned it a special place in railway history:

The story of how, in spite of its restricted facilities, and in spite of so many hampering circumstances and conditions, the Highland Railway carried so immense a traffic, and rendered services of inestimable value in the prosecution of the war, is one that reflects the highest credit upon the responsible railway officers and the staff from whom they received such loyal and strenuous support. It is the story of a comparatively small railway, little known to the vast majority of English people, but one that accomplished a task distinguished even among the many striking records of what Transport achieved in a World Conflict that has well been called a Railway War.

RIGHT One of the famous Jellicoe Specials steaming up the line.

THE ARMISTICE CARRIAGE

On 11 November 1918, the guns finally fell silent on the Western Front. And fittingly, after four years of war on the tracks, the momentous agreement that put a stop to the violence was signed in a railway carriage.

This historic wagon formed part of a train used by Marshal Ferdinand Foch, one of the most senior French generals, who in April 1918 had been made General-in-Chief of the Allie Armies. He travelled the front line by rail, in a special train complete with sleeping, eating and working quarters. Its main office had originally been a dining car, built in 1913 as Wagon 2419D by the Compagnie Internationale des Wagons-Lits – the Belgian firm famous for its luxurious international express trains. These glamorous sleepers had traversed the Continent in the years of pre-war decadence, whisking well-heeled Europeans across borders in style. Little could these Belle Epoque travellers have imagined that one

LEFT Marshal Ferdinand Foch, General-in-Chief of the Allied Armies.

of their comfortable restaurant cars was to play a starring role in world history.

By the autumn of 1918, with the failure of their planned offensive all too apparent, the Germans felt they had no option but to seek a ceasefire. As the Allied advance continued to forge ahead, one by one Germany's allies among the Central Powers dropped out of the fighting. Meanwhile, on the German home front, scarcities of food and other essentials were reaching crisis point, and as the prospect of military victory receded, the threat of revolution reared its head.

In October, the Germans opened negotiations with the Allies, initially brokered by the United States. As messages flew back and forth between the parties, the Germans were initially optimistic that they could win some concessions. But as conditions on the battlefield and the home front continued to deteriorate, it became increasingly clear that they would have to settle for a ceasefire at almost any price – or risk the collapse of the German state. By early November, there was a renewed sense of urgency. On the Western Front, under continued pressure from the Allied advance, morale amongst the troops was crumbling. Sailors in Kiel had already mutinied and were calling for revolution across the rest of the country. Amid this mounting chaos, on 6 November the Germans requested a meeting with Marshal Foch.

To stage the rendezvous, a secluded spot in the Compiègne forest, between Amiens and Reims, was chosen. It was far from prying eyes, yet had easy railway access thanks to lines originally built for French railway guns. The two sides would come face to face in the narrow confines of Wagon 2419D.

On 8 November, a group of German representatives under French escort arrived by train at the meeting place, and for the next three days Foch's railway carriage bore witness to the secret talks.

The terms proposed by the Allies were punishing. Germany would have to withdraw from all occupied territory, including Alsace-Lorraine, which had been in German hands since the Franco-Prussian War of 1871. It was required to surrender vast quantities of military equipment, including thousands of railway locomotives, and submit its High Seas Fleet to internment in a neutral or Allied port. But by this point the Germans were in no position to push back. As the streets of German cities seethed with unrest, there was mounting pressure on the Kaiser to abdicate. On 9 November, he succumbed, fleeing to Holland as the German Empire was soon declared a republic.

Two days later, at 5 a.m. on 11 November, the armistice agreement was finally signed. Due to come into effect six hours later, at the eleventh hour of the eleventh day of the eleventh month, the document committed both sides to a thirty-six-day ceasefire. In Britain, the terms of the agreement were described by David Lloyd George in the House of Commons: 'Thus at eleven o'clock this morning came to an end the cruellest and most terrible War that has ever scourged mankind. I hope we may say that thus, this fateful morning, came to an end all wars.'

Lloyd George's optimism proved unfounded. But in the short term at least, the temporary armistice held. In 1919, after lengthy negotiations, it was formalized into a peace agreement with the Treaty of Versailles. As a reminder of the Allied triumph, the 'Armistice Wagon' as it became known was displayed in Paris for a time, then,

Photographie prise le 11 Novembre 1918 à 7 h. 30, au moment où le Maréchal Foch part pour Paris remettre au gouvernement français le texte de l'Armistice qui vient d'être signé avec l'Allemagne.

1. Maréchal FOCH.
2. Amiral Sir R. WEMYSS.
3. Général WEYGAND.
4. Contre-amiral G. HOPE.
5. Captain MARRIOTT.
6. Général DESTICKER.
7. Capitaine de MIERRY.
8. Commandant RIEDINGER.
9. Officier-Interprète LAPERCHE

in 1927, it was returned to the Compiègne forest. There, the tracks used by the Allied and German trains were preserved in a clearing, overlooked by a heroic statue of Marshal Foch, and the carriage itself was installed in a museum building as a permanent memorial. But that wasn't the end of its role in world history.

For many in Germany, the armistice and the subsequent peace settlement were bitterly resented. Pre-eminent among those who wanted revenge was First World War veteran Adolf Hitler. In June 1940, in the wake of his crushing invasion of France, Hitler insisted that the

French signed the armistice in the exact same spot as the ceasefire of 1914 – in the very same railway carriage that had witnessed Germany's humiliation in 1918. Once the French had agreed to the division of the country between the Axis Powers and the Vichy government, the forest clearing was desecrated and the wagon itself carried off to Germany.

There it stayed until April 1945 when, as the Allies advanced and German defeat drew closer, members of the SS deliberately set fire to the carriage in order to prevent it falling into Allied hands. The burnt remains were buried and hidden, not to be rediscovered until after the reunification of Germany in 1990.

But despite the destruction of Wagon 2419D, the clearing in the Compiègne forest had not lost its symbolic power. It was painstakingly rebuilt as a memorial, and in 1950 a replacement 'Armistice Wagon' was found. It was another Compagnie Internationale des Wagons-Lits dining car, built in the same consignment as the 1918 original. The contents of Foch's carriage had been preserved at the start of the Second World War, and now they were arranged in their new home exactly as they had been for the fateful meeting. Today, the replica armistice carriage can still be visited in the museum in the clearing near Compiègne, which remains a place of pilgrimage for people seeking to understand the cataclysmic events of the First World War.

As the story of Foch's railway carriage illustrates, the conflict was to cast a long shadow over the twentieth century. And as Europe struggled to come to terms with its aftermath, the railways continued to play a leading role.

CHAPTER 5

RAILWAYS
AND
REMEMBRANCE

The railways' war work didn't end with the armistice. Before they could get back to a peacetime footing, the long process of demobilization had to be completed, with some 2 million troops on the Western Front returned to their homes. As the railways took the strain of this extra traffic, they carried not just military personnel but also more than 100,000 horses and millions of army greatcoats, sent back to army ordnance depots by soldiers grateful for the £1 payment they received in return.

In July of that year, after the Treaty of Versailles was signed and peace finally confirmed, packed trains brought thousands of visitors to London to take part in a 'Peace Day' celebration. But even as the jubilant crowds poured into the capital, Britain faced the sombre task of counting its dead.

REMEMBERING RAILWAYMEN – A SERVICE AT ST PAUL'S

Our comrades were men who had remained at their posts faithful to the end; our brother railwaymen who had booked their last train . . . waved the last flag, and steamed away from this railway life into . . . eternity.

. . . Slowly we filed out into the afternoon sunshine, to the warm, real world, to the roar and animation of the city life, and then, back to the railway stations we bent our steps.

An account of the Railwaymen's Memorial Service at St Paul's, published in the *South Western Railway Magazine* in June 1919.

It is estimated that almost 9.5 million servicemen worldwide laid down their lives in the Great War, some 723,000 of them from the United Kingdom. And among their number were nearly 19,000 British railwaymen – around a tenth of the 186,000 who had answered the call. As the dust settled on the battlefields, thoughts turned to remembrance. The first Armistice Day commemorations in Britain were held in November 1919, but even before that the railwaymen of Great Britain and Ireland had been honoured with their own memorial service.

On Wednesday, 14 May 1919, a congregation of 4,000 gathered at St Paul's in the presence of King George V. The great and the good of the railway establishment were there, alongside bereaved families and ordinary railway workers. Even the music was provided by an orchestra of railway employees, including women – a novelty later described by Pratt as:

> *. . . a graceful recognition, not only of the part that women had played in the winning of the war, but, more especially, of the fact that it was their readiness to take up railway work in a great variety of forms which had enabled many of those in whose memory the service was being held to join the service and make the sacrifice of their lives for the Great Cause in which they fought.*

RIGHT St Paul's Cathedral – site of the first memorial service for railwaymen lost in the First World War.

Each member of the congregation was presented with an Order of Service containing not just details of the ceremony itself but also a list of the 18,957 railwaymen then known to have been killed in the line of duty. Listed in alphabetical order by railway company, each man has a brief entry – his name, pre-war railway grade and military rank – and, until recently, little more information was available. But seven years ago, a railwayman and Territorial Army officer set himself the daunting task of uncovering the personal history of each and every one of the railways' war dead.

Jeremy Higgins was inspired to begin his research when, returning to work on the railways from a six-month stint in Iraq, he noticed the Great Western Railway's First World War memorial at Leamington Spa station and began to wonder about the men behind the names. He decided to pick one at random and see if

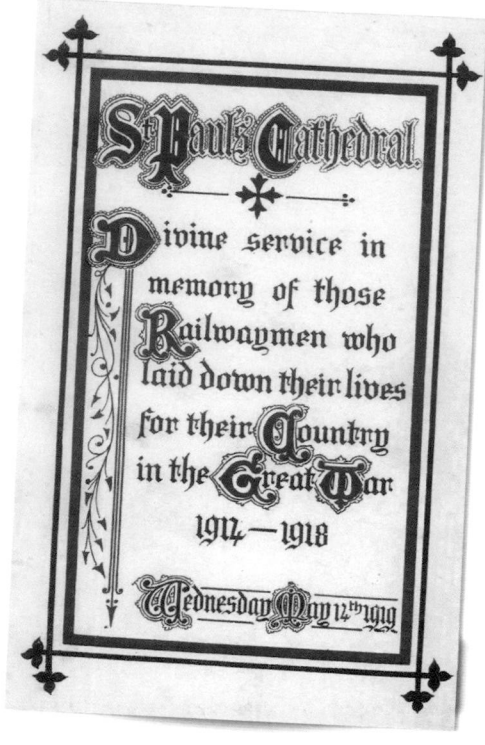

ABOVE The cover of the Order of Service for the memorial service held at St Paul's. It lists the names of 18,957 railwaymen.

it was possible to find out more about him. Success spurred him on to further research, and Higgins has now uncovered the stories of 12,500 fallen railway workers, many of which feature in his book *Great War Railwaymen.*

By tracing these men's stories, Higgins has built up a picture of the railways' human contribution to the war effort. What's striking is that while many lent their skills to the railway war in construction or operating companies, railwaymen ventured well beyond their comfort zone on tracks over land. Also at home at sea and even in the air, railwaymen sacrificed their lives as part of all the armed services.

In the Royal Navy, one of the earliest railway casualties Higgins has found was George Coleman. On the outbreak of war, it appears that Coleman was a naval reservist employed by the Midland Railway at St Pancras as a Dining-Car Attendant. By September 1914, he had joined the naval cruiser HMS *Cressy* as a Steward, a junior rank equivalent to Able-Seaman. While the setting was very different from a railway dining car, many of Coleman's day-to-day duties – which would have included serving meals to the officers and cleaning up after them – would have been reassuringly familiar. But his naval career was to prove short-lived, as Coleman was involved in one of the war's most shocking naval disasters.

The *Cressy* was one of a group of old and rather decrepit cruisers brought back into service for the war, and doubts had been cast on whether they should be at sea at all. Nevertheless, early in the morning of 22 September, the *Cressy* was out on patrol in the North Sea, together with two other cruisers of the same class – the *Aboukir* and the *Hogue*. As dawn broke, the weather was clear and all seemed well, but, unbeknown to the sailors, they had been spotted by a solitary German submarine.

It was a stroke of extremely bad luck. The U-boat, captained by Otto Weddigen, had been sent out to attack troopships bound for Belgium but had been forced off course by bad weather. When it crossed paths with the cruisers, Weddigen seized the opportunity and fired a torpedo at the *Aboukir*.

The missile struck home at around 6.30 a.m., and soon the *Aboukir* was sinking. Then, as the *Cressy* and *Hogue* steamed to the aid of the victims, they too were picked off by U-9. The *Cressy* was the last to sink, at 7.55 a.m. In around ninety minutes, 36,000 tons of British warships and nearly 1,400 lives had been lost. Twenty-five-year-old George Coleman was one of at least thirty-seven railwaymen among them.

This wasn't the war's first successful submarine attack – that had taken place three weeks earlier, when the *Pathfinder* was torpedoed near the mouth of the Firth of Forth. But the sinking of the *Cressy*, *Hogue* and *Aboukir* by just one small U-boat scandalized the nation and forced Britain to treat the U-boat threat much more seriously.

The First World War wasn't the first time that submarines had been used, but the technology came of age during the conflict. The war also saw air power make its debut as a significant tool in battle. The Royal Flying Corps and the Royal Naval Air Service were the forerunners of the Royal Air Force, formed in April 1918, and it soon became clear that technically proficient railway workers could be an asset in the air war. Railwaymen were among the pioneers who pushed the boundaries of aerial combat and, according to Higgins, at least thirty railwaymen died in the air.

Among them was flying ace Flight Sub-Lieutenant Harold Day. Born in rural South Wales, in peacetime he was employed at the Great Western Railway's Swindon works, and when war broke out he lent his skills to the Royal Naval Air Service. He trained as a pilot and flew Sopwith Triplanes and later Camels with great success, shooting

Kapitänleutnant Weddigen.

down a total of eleven enemy aircraft. His death in February 1918 came not at the hands of the Germans but as a result of a fatal accident when his plane suddenly plummeted to the ground, probably because of technical failure.

Day was just twenty years old when he died and was posthumously awarded the Distinguished Service Cross 'in recognition of the skill and determination shown by him in aerial combats'.

Jeremy Higgins' research also shines a light on some of the war's less well-remembered theatres. In Basra in Iraq, where Higgins himself served in 2003, stands a memorial to more than 40,000 British and Empire servicemen with no known grave. They lost their lives in what was known as the Mesopotamian Campaign, and among their number were at least 102 railwaymen.

Mesopotamia was an area along the banks of the rivers Euphrates and Tigris, most of which is in modern-day Iraq. In the early twentieth century, the region was under Ottoman rule, and the Ottoman Empire entered the war on Germany's side in October 1914. The first British

ABOVE An image of the torpedo attack by Otto Weddigen's U-9 on 22 September 1914.

RIGHT Flight Sub-Lieutenant Harold Day, one of at least thirty railwaymen who died in the air during the First World War.

soldiers, joined by Indian forces, arrived in Mesopotamia in November to fight Turkish troops. Advancing north from the Persian Gulf coast towards Baghdad, they at first enjoyed some success but soon started to encounter difficulties, caused in part by a lack of supplies – the British Empire forces were entirely reliant on river transport to move materiel to the battle zone, and not enough was getting through.

By November 1915, the supply lines were stretched to breaking point, and a drawn battle at Ctesiphon, about twenty miles south-east of Baghdad, checked the British advance. Britain's problems culminated in the siege of Kut-al-Amara, where Turkish forces encircling 13,000 British and Indian troops managed to fend off a series of relief efforts. The siege lasted for months and witnessed the first ever airdrop of food aid and other supplies. Eventually, in April 1916, the besieged British force was forced to surrender.

It was a humiliating moment for Britain, but the following year a fresh advance was planned, and railways were to prove vital to its success. Indeed, the *Railway Gazette* later claimed that 'it was solely the rapid development of railways that enabled [troops] to pursue the campaign to a victorious conclusion'. Starting in 1916, an ambitious programme

of track construction began. With extreme heat in summer and frequent flooding in spring when the snow melted in the mountains, the railway builders faced very different challenges from their comrades on the Western Front. Nevertheless, in just over two years around 1,000 miles of new railway tracks were laid, ensuring the steady flow of supplies to the troops.

By 1917, British and Indian troops were moving forward once again, and in March of that year troops conquered Baghdad. Just north of the city on 29 March, the 5th (Service) Battalion, the Wiltshire Regiment, took part in an engagement against some 4,000 Turkish troops. Of the twenty-eight members of the battalion who died that day, three were railwaymen: Private William Bates and Corporal Charles Wiffen, both Clerks from

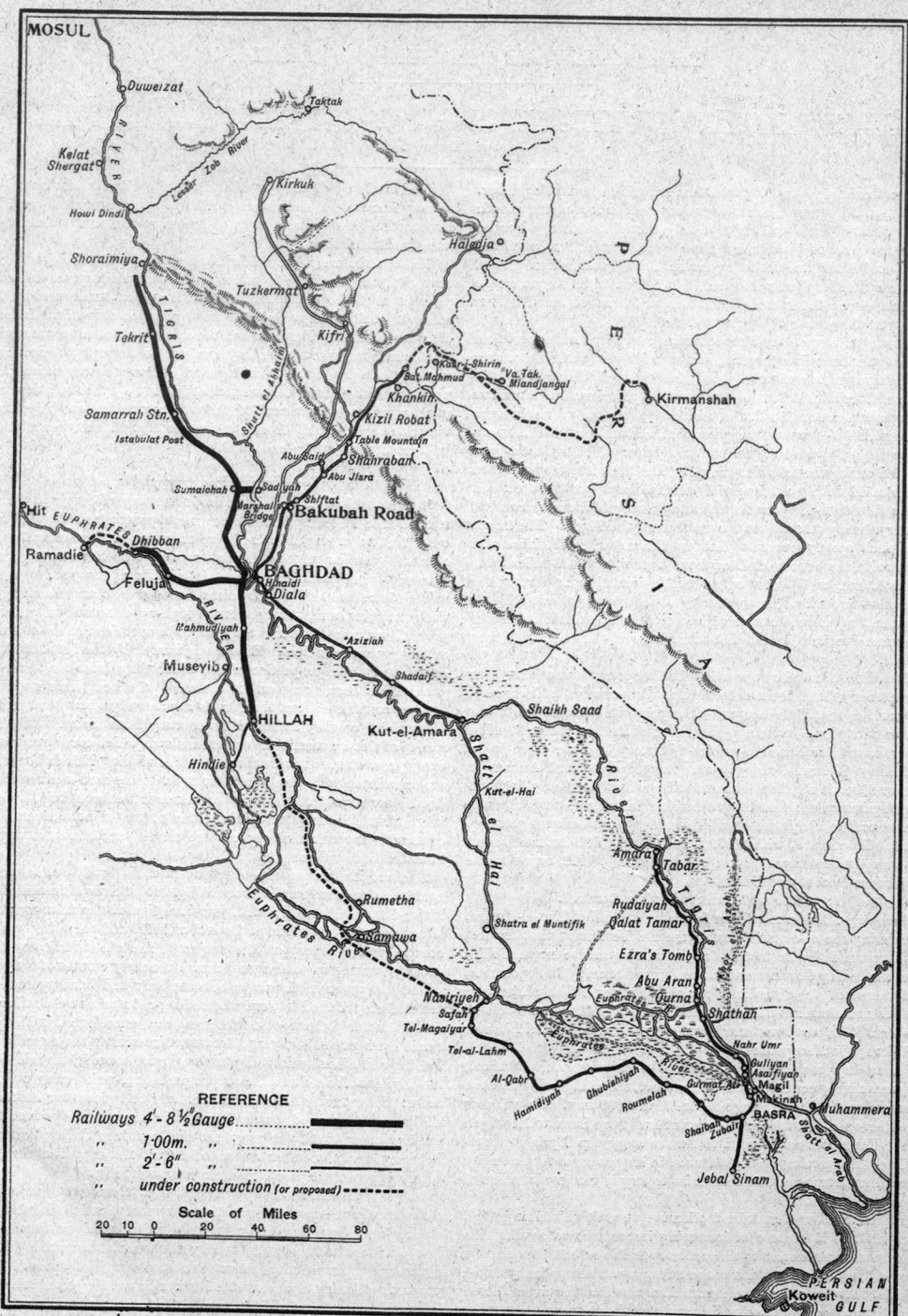

Fig. 34.—Railways Constructed in Mesopotamia during the War.

LEFT A map produced for the *Railway Gazette's Special War Transportation number*, showing the extensive network of railways laid in Mesopotamia.

BELOW The obelisk at Euston station.

the Great Eastern Railway, and Private Edward Gulley, a Carriage Fitter formerly employed by the Great Western.

Delving into the personal stories of railwaymen who lost their lives in this first global conflict reveals the extraordinary range of combatants' experiences. Workers returning to the familiar world of the signal box and the ticket office might have spent the preceding years trudging through desert or lurking beneath the waves in an Allied submarine; wading through Flanders mud or soaring through the skies in an early fighter plane.

For the unlucky ones who lay where they had fallen, once the strains of the St Paul's service died away the railway companies set about creating more lasting memorials. Among Britain's 54,000 monuments to the war dead, some of the most impressive are found in railway stations, where the powerful railway companies built tributes to their fallen employees. At Paddington, Great Western Railway employees are commemorated by a simple statue of a soldier that presides over Platform 1, while at Euston the London and North Western Railway commissioned a 45-foot obelisk, flanked by four bronze figures. At London Waterloo, the memorial was built into the very facade of the station itself, then being reconstructed. When the building finally opened in 1922, around the main entrance was a vast, ornate arch, designed by architect J. R. Scott and featuring Bellona, Roman Goddess of War, alongside figures of Peace and Victory, and crowned by Britannia bearing a torch of Liberty. Today, these memorials are the site of commemorative services on Armistice Day, and even the hustle and bustle of the capital's busiest stations is stilled into silence for two minutes at 11 o'clock on 11 November every year.

W & K   THE LONDON & NORTH WESTERN RLY., MEMORIAL
Erected in Commemoration of the 3719 Employees who fell in the Great War
UNVEILED BY EARL HAIG OCTOBER 21st 1921

RAILWAY HEROES OF THE LONDON AND NORTH WESTERN RAILWAY

By the end of the war, at least six railwaymen had received the highest award for gallantry on the battlefield: the Victoria Cross (VC). Three of them were employees of the same company, the London and North Western Railway (L&NWR), and after the armistice the firm honoured its heroes by giving their names to three of its 'Claughton' class locomotives.

The *Lance Corporal J. A. Christie VC* was named after a former Parcels Clerk at Euston who served in Gallipoli and Palestine, where he won his award for 'most conspicuous bravery when, after a position had been captured, the enemy immediately made counter and bombing attacks'. Alone and completely exposed, Christie counter-attacked, bombing the enemy until the position was clear, showing 'the greatest coolness and a total disregard for his own safety'. Christie survived the war but did not return to the railway.

Ernest Sykes, a Platelayer before the war, was the man behind the 'Claughton' class *Private E. Sykes VC*. He won his award at Arras in 1917, and his citation praises his 'contempt of danger' when, under heavy machine-gun fire, he 'went forward and brought back four wounded men. He made a fifth journey and remained out under conditions that appeared to be certain death, until he had bandaged all those who were too badly wounded to be moved.'

When the fighting finished, Ernest Sykes did go back to the L&NWR, as did his comrade Wilfred Wood, for whom the *Private W. Wood VC* was named.

Won in Italy on 28 October 1918, Wood's VC was one of the last to be awarded in the conflict, after he 'captured an enemy machine-gun nest and caused 140 men to surrender'. After the war, Wood became a Fireman, while Sykes was eventually promoted to Guard. According to Jeremy Higgins, on at least one occasion the two Victoria Cross winners found themselves sharing a shift on board the same train.

The L&NWR also created a special remembrance locomotive named *Patriot* – a moving memorial to the dead. In the 1930s, by which time the L&NWR had become part of the London, Midland and Scottish (LMS) Railway, the 'Claughton' class was withdrawn and the name 'Patriot' was transferred to the first of the new design that replaced it. This model became known as the 'Patriot' class, and Sykes' and Wood's nameplates were also transferred to two of the new engines, which remained in service until the 1960s.

The idea of the memorial engine has recently been revived by a group of enthusiasts who have launched a project to build a new 'Patriot' class locomotive. By 2018, it should be ready to run in steam on the main line once again, named *The Unknown Warrior* in honour of all those who died a century before.

A RAILWAY MARTYR RETURNS

The vast majority of the First World War's victims were servicemen. But the conflict claimed civilian lives too. On the railways, workers fell victim to air raids on several occasions, including ten railway staff who died in a single attack on Liverpool Street station on 13 June 1917. But perhaps surprisingly, the railway industry's most famous civilian victim lost his life after an incident at sea.

Britain's thriving pre-war railway companies employed not just engine drivers, tracklayers and station staff but also ship's captains, stewards and dock workers. Back in the nineteenth century, the companies whose tracks served Britain's coastal ports had realized there were great advantages in offering customers a seamless service even beyond Britain's shores and began purchasing passenger steamers to complement their fleets of locomotives. By the Edwardian era, 14 English and Scottish railway companies owned between them 218 steamships, extending the reach of the British railway network to Ireland, the Scottish Isles and Continental Europe.

The Great Eastern Railway's (GER's) maritime operation was particularly impressive. In 1883, they kick-started a dramatic expansion of the Port of Harwich in Essex by building their own dedicated quay at Parkeston. By the eve of the First World War, Harwich had grown into Britain's premier passenger port, running frequent services to Belgium and Holland. As well as passengers, the GER carried a sizeable traffic in freight, and in 1914 the captain of one of its cargo ships, the *Newmarket,* was forty-two-year-old Charles Algernon Fryatt, a sailor of over twenty years' experience.

ABOVE Captain Charles Algernon Fryatt – an experienced civilian sailor who was captured and shot by the Germans.

LEFT Sykes' nameplate.

With the outbreak of hostilities, more than half the railways' ships were requisitioned by the War Office, including the GER's *Newmarket*, and were put to work as troop carriers, minesweepers, convoy ships and coal boats. Most passenger services to the Continent were cancelled, but the GER decided to try to maintain its link to neutral Holland – a vital route into Britain for Dutch food imports. And so Captain Fryatt was set to work plying this route under the strain of wartime conditions.

Negotiating minefields and coping without normal aids to navigation such as buoys made for challenging crossings. But it was U-boats that posed the biggest threat to merchant ships. Quite early on in the war, the Germans had decided that their best chance of severing Britain's trade links lay with submarine warfare, and sticking to military targets wasn't enough. With the Allied blockade successfully strangling German supply routes, Germany wanted to fight back by threatening merchant shipping. So, in early 1915 it declared the seas around Britain a war zone, warning all merchant ships that they entered these waters at their peril.

This announcement of unrestricted submarine warfare turned the traditional rules of engagement at sea on their head. Formerly, merchant vessels had to be given time to get their crews and passengers to safety before they could be sunk. In return, civilian boats were supposed to submit to military challenges. But now British merchant seamen knew they could be torpedoed without warning, and they were encouraged by the Admiralty to do all in their power to evade U-boat attacks.

Captain Fryatt met his first submarine on 2 March 1915 and managed to outrun it – though only by pushing his ship the *Wrexham* so hard that its funnels were blackened and burnt when it arrived at Rotterdam. He won acclaim for his efforts, but it was a U-boat encounter a few weeks later that sealed Fryatt's fate. On 28 March, he was captaining GER ship the *Brussels,* en route from Harwich to Rotterdam, when he was ordered to stop by German submarine U-33. But he refused. This time there was no chance of escape, so instead Fryatt made a course straight for the U-boat, forcing it to dive. Once again, Fryatt had taken on the U-boat menace and won.

Back home, Captain Fryatt was hailed as a hero. He was congratulated by the Admiralty, who even presented him with a gold watch for his bravery in the face of the enemy. But the Germans saw things very differently. What Britain regarded as a valiant and entirely legitimate act of self-defence was in Germany interpreted as the action of a *franc-tireur* – a civilian acting unlawfully as a combatant in war. On 22 June the following year, Fryatt was at the helm of the *Brussels* once again – his ninety-eighth trip since the start of the war. He was carrying refugees and cargo from the Hook of Holland to Harwich when he was intercepted by German destroyers and taken prisoner. A month later, he was convicted of having committed an act of guerrilla warfare and condemned to death. Within hours of receiving his sentence, Fryatt had been shot.

News of Fryatt's execution was met with outrage back in Britain. The British authorities denounced it as judicial murder, and it joined the sinking of the *Lusitania* and the burning of Leuven/Louvain in the public mind as yet another example of German atrocities. Already a hero, Fryatt had become a martyr, and when the war ended his family and the staff of the GER campaigned to have his remains repatriated from Belgium and reburied in Britain.

In July 1919, that wish was granted. Fryatt's body was exhumed from its grave in Bruges and taken to Brussels to lie in state in the Grand Place before travelling to Antwerp to board a British destroyer bound for Dover. Then, once safely on British soil, the precious cargo was entrusted to a rather special railway van.

Built earlier that year at the South Eastern and Chatham Railway's Ashford works, the prototype Passenger Luggage Van number 132 had been intended to carry wealthy passengers' trunks and suitcases, but by the time of Fryatt's repatriation it had already earned a pedigree as a vehicle fit for heroes. It was completed in spring 1919, at the very moment when the railways were seeking a suitable vehicle to carry the remains of nurse Edith Cavell. She had been executed by the Germans in 1915 for helping British prisoners escape from occupied Belgium, and she became the war's most famous female casualty. British propaganda

ABOVE A portait of Nurse Cavell.

RIGHT An allegorical picture printed in a British newspaper soon after Edith Cavell's death. Her execution was a common theme for Allied propaganda.

helped cement her reputation as a martyr, and after the armistice it was decided her body should be brought home. As the most modern vehicle in the South Eastern and Chatham's fleet, Van 132 was quickly fitted out as a Chapel of Rest. It was waved on by huge crowds lining the route to London, where the nurse was given a memorial service in Westminster Abbey.

When, two months later, Fryatt's remains were also brought home, the Cavell Van, as it had become known, seemed the obvious choice. It carried Fryatt's coffin from Dover to Charing Cross, from where it was taken to St Paul's for a special service attended by railwaymen and sailors from across the country.

LEFT After his remains were brought home from Belgium in 1919, Captain Fryatt was honoured with a service in St Paul's Cathedral.

Van 132 had earned a special place in railway history. But Fryatt's final journey wasn't the end of its story. Before it returned to its normal railway duties, it was destined to carry a third and final war hero. His journey in November 1920 was the most solemnly celebrated of them all, yet he remains anonymous.

The idea of commemorating the death of an Unknown Warrior was born out of one of the most heartbreaking features of the war – the huge number of fallen soldiers whose bodies were never recovered or whose remains were found but never identified. By the 1930s, the Western Front was home to 180,000 unnamed graves, while around 300,000 names were engraved on Memorials to the Missing. The grave of an unknown soldier was intended to provide a symbolic focus for the many families unable to follow the normal rituals of grief.

From four bodies exhumed from battlefields across the Western Front, one was selected and placed in a specially built coffin, hewn from oak grown at Hampton Court Palace. It was brought from France on destroyer HMS *Verdun*, before being transferred to Van 132 and carried to Victoria. There, it spent the night under guard on the platform – now commemorated by a plaque in the station – before commencing its solemn final journey. The coffin paused on Whitehall, where King George V unveiled the permanent Cenotaph, then proceeded to Westminster Abbey. Carried by pallbearers including Admirals, Field Marshals and Generals, the Unknown Warrior was saluted by a guard of honour made up of 100 Victoria Cross winners before being laid to rest in the same hallowed ground as many former kings and queens.

Within a week, more than a million men and women had flocked to Westminster to pay their respects, and the Unknown Warrior's grave remains one of the most-visited war graves in the world. Today, people can also commemorate the Warrior's last journey by visiting the Kent and East Sussex Railway heritage line, the current home of Van 132. The railway acquired the van back in 1992, by which time it had long languished in storage, its proud history forgotten. But the volunteers who run the railway gradually pieced together its remarkable story and successfully raised funds to restore it to its 1920 condition. In 2010, the restored carriage was finally unveiled, complete with a replica of the Unknown Warrior's coffin, built by volunteers at the Kent and East Sussex Railway and fitted with ironwork made in North Wales by the grandson of the original craftsman.

LEFT AND BELOW
Van 132 has been lovingly restored by the volunteers of the Kent and East Sussex Railway heritage line.

RAILWAY PILGRIMS TO THE WESTERN FRONT –
BATTLEFIELD TOURISM IS BORN

Every year, hundreds of thousands of people visit the battlefields of France and Belgium. Schoolchildren are taken on group tours. Descendants pay homage to fathers, grandfathers and great-grandfathers killed in action. And holidaymakers pause between beach trips, ice creams and museum visits for a moment of sombre reflection. But the idea of battlefield tourism is not new. Indeed, it was born even before the war had ended. Michelin Guides published a book describing the key sites in France in 1917, and almost as soon as hostilities ended veterans and bereaved families began visiting the places where their friends, comrades and loved ones had fallen.

The railways were quick to get in on the act. As early as 1920, *The Times* was advertising 'Tours to the British battlefields in France, arranged by the South-Eastern and Chatham Railway Company, in association with the Societé Française des Auto-Mails . . . daily from London'. Clearly aimed at the well-heeled, the ticket included first-class travel, hotels and transfers – but at £15 15s, around twelve times the average weekly wage for a labourer, the price was beyond the reach of most families.

In 1923, the charitable organization St Barnabas Hostels began arranging subsidized and free (for those most in need) battlefield tours, taking up to 930 people at a time by train to France and Belgium. But it was the British Legion that arranged the most impressive post-war mass railway pilgrimage. In August 1928, ten years after the 'turning of the tide' in the Allies' favour on the Western Front, around 11,000 veterans and family members converged on Ypres in what was dubbed even at the time an 'Epic Pilgrimage'.

Central to pulling off this ambitious scheme was a complicated railway timetable, devised under the leadership of the pilgrimage's dedicated 'Transport Officer' Major W. Daniell. Indeed, the trains provided the central organizing principle for the event. For the duration of the trip, the pilgrims were divided into trainloads of 500 or so people, with each group identified by a particular letter that its members wore on a badge.

With echoes of the initial mobilization of the British Expeditionary Force fourteen years earlier, the first challenge was to bring pilgrims from across the country by rail to the ports, ready to cross to the Continent.

TRAIN PARTY.	AUGUST 4TH. (Meals.)	AUGUST 5TH. (Meals.)	AUGUST 6TH. (Meals.)	AUGUST 7TH. (Meals.)	AUGUST 8TH — YPRES CONCENTRATION — Arrivals.	Place of Assembly and Meals there.	Arrive back Assembly Place after Ceremony.	Time of Concentration for Entrainment.
A B.E.S.L. and Reserves	D. London 16.40 D. Dover 19.30 A. Calais 21.00 Supper D. Calais 22.00	A. Amiens 01.05 Lunch (St. Roch) Billets	D. Amiens 09.30 A. Beaucourt 10.20 Lunch & A. Beaucourt 17.10 Tea A. Amiens 17.45	D. Amiens 08.50 A. Vimy 10.00 Lunch & A. Vimy 15.55 Tea A. Amiens 17.15	D. Amiens 06.45 A. Ypres 09.56	War Graves Depot. Breakfast. Lunch. Tea. Supper.	14.00	19.50
B HOME COUNTIES	D. London 16.55 D. Dover 19.30 A. Calais 21.00 Supper D. Calais 22.10	A. Amiens 01.15 Lunch (St. Roch) Billets	D. Amiens 08.50 A. Vimy 10.00 Lunch & A. Vimy 15.55 Tea A. Amiens 17.15	D. Amiens 09.30 A. Beaucourt 10.20 Lunch & D. Beaucourt 17.10 Tea A. Amiens 17.45	D. Amiens 06.55 A. Ypres 10.15	Caserne Inf. Breakfast. Lunch Tea.	13.00	17.00
C WALES	Via Reading	A. Dover 03.00 D. Dover 05.00 Tea A. Calais 06.30 Breakfast D. Calais 07.30 A. Tourcoing 09.40 Lunch Bs.	D. Tourcoing 09.25 A. Vimy 10.57 Lunch & A. Vimy 16.43 Tea A. Tourcoing 17.56	D. Tourcoing 09.20 A. Beaucourt 11.10 Lunch & D. Beaucourt 16.40 Tea A. Tourcoing 18.34	D. Tourcoing 06.15 A. Ypres 07.45	Ecole Garcons. Breakfast. Lunch Tea.	13.16	15.10
D S. WESTERN	Via Guildford — Supper Tn	A. Dover 03.15 D. Dover 05.00 Tea A. Calais 06.30 Breakfast D. Calais 07.40 A. St. Omer 08.20 Lunch Bs.	D. St. Omer 09.05 A. Vimy 10.35 Lunch & A. Vimy 16.25 Tea A. St. Omer 17.55	D. St. Omer 08.05 A. Beaucourt 10.40 Lunch & D. Beaucourt 17.15 Tea A. St. Omer 19.20	D. St. Omer 06.50 A. Ypres 09.20	Ecole Moyen. Breakfast. Lunch. Tea.	13.08	15.22
E EAST MIDLAND I.	D. Kensington 04.05 (5th Aug)	A. Dover 06.30 Breakfast D. Dover 09.00 A. Calais 10.30 D. Calais 11.30 A. Valenciennes 14.00 Meat Tea Bs.	D. Valenciennes 09.45 A. Vimy 11.10 Lunch & A. Vimy 16.15 Tea A. Valenciennes 17.40	D. Valenciennes 09.45 A. Beaucourt 11.10 Lunch & D. Beaucourt 17.05 Tea A. Valenciennes 17.40	D. Valenciennes 07.00 A. Ypres 09.22	Ecole Filles. Breakfast. Lunch Tea.	13.48	18.30
F METROPOLITAN II. & S. EASTERN II.		D. London 12.02 D. Dover 14.45 A. Calais 16.15 Tea D. Calais 17.10 A. H. Lietard 19.25	D. H. Lietard 09.35 A. Beaucourt 11.00 Lunch & D. Beaucourt 17.35 Tea A. H. Lietard 18.55	D. H. Lietard 09.50 A. Vimy 10.20 Lunch & D. Vimy 15.50 Tea A. H. Lietard 16.15	D. H. Lietard 07.25 A. Ypres 09.30	Ecole Moyen. Breakfast. Lunch Tea.	13.44	18.45
G METROPOLITAN I.		D. London 08.15 D. Dover 10.30 A. Calais 12.00 Lunch D. Calais 12.40 A. Arras 15.00 Meat Tea Br.	D. Arras 10.50 A. Beaucourt 11.20 Lunch & D. Beaucourt 16.50 Tea A. Arras 17.20	D. Arras 10.00 A. Vimy 10.15 Lunch & D. Vimy 16.50 Tea A. Arras 17.05	D. Arras 06.30 A. Ypres 08.48	Convent de la St. Famille. Breakfast. Lunch. Tea. Supper.	14.04	20.05
H IRISH	D. Kensington 06.15 Supper Tn. (5th Aug).	A. Dover 08.45 Breakfast D. Dover 10.30 A. Calais 12.00 Lunch D. Calais 12.50 A. Lens 15.50 Tea Bs.	D. Lens 10.15 A. Beaucourt 11.10 Lunch & D. Beaucourt 16.30 Tea A. Lens 17.30	D. Lens 09.50 A. Vimy 10.00 Lunch & D. Vimy 16.55 Tea A. Lens 17.05	D. Lens 06.25 A. Ypres 08.33	Convent Rousbrugge. Breakfast. Lunch Tea	13.20	15.34
I WEST MIDLAND I.	D. Kensington 04.20 (5th Aug.)	A. Dover 06.45 Breakfast D. Dover 09.00 A. Calais 10.30 D. Calais 11.40 A. Amiens 15.20 Meat Tea Bs	D. Amiens 09.25 A. Vimy 10.45 Lunch & D. Vimy 16.05 Tea A. Amiens 17.35	D. Amiens 09.25 A. Beaucourt 10.10 Lunch & D. Beaucourt 16.00 Tea A. Amiens 16.40	D. Amiens 07.05 A. Ypres 10.25	Caserne Inf. Breakfast. Lunch Tea.	13.04	15.47
J SOUTH-EASTERN I.		*D. London 12.15 Lunch Tn D. Dover 14.45 A. Calais 16.15 Tea D. Calais 16.50 A. Douai 19.20	D. Douai 09.15 A. Beaucourt 10.05 Lunch & D. Beaucourt 17.05 Tea A. Douai 18.00	D. Douai 09.30 A. Vimy 10.08 Lunch & D. Vimy 16.25 Tea A. Douai 17.05	D. Douai 06.20 A. Ypres 08.30	Convent Rousbrugge. Breakfast. Lunch. Tea.	13.36	17.15
K NORTH-EASTERN		12.30 D. Kensington 12.40 Lunch Tn D. Dover 16.30 Tea A. Calais 18.00 D. Calais 19.00 Supper A. Arras 21.20	D. Arras 10.00 A. Vimy 10.15 Lunch & D. Vimy 16.50 Tea A. Arras 17.05	D. Arras 10.50 A. Beaucourt 11.20 Lunch & D. Beaucourt 16.50 Tea A. Arras 17.20	D. Arras 06.45 A. Ypres 09.32	Ecole Garcons. Breakfast. Lunch. Tea.	13.32	16.55
L EX. S. WOMEN & WOMEN'S SECTION III (2nd Class)		D. London 13.35 Lunch Tn D. Dover 16.30 Tea A. Calais 18.00 D. Calais 18.28 A. Roubaix 20.55 Supper Bs	D. Roubaix 09.55 A. Beaucourt 11.40 Lunch & D. Beaucourt 17.50 Tea A. Roubaix 19.38	D. Roubaix 09.30 A. Vimy 10.57 Lunch & D. Vimy 16.43 Tea A. Roubaix 17.50	D. Roubaix 07.15 A. Ypres 08.45	Ecole Filles. Breakfast. Lunch. Tea.	13.56	17.19
M WOMEN'S SECTION I (2nd Class)		D. London 16.20 D. Dover 19.15 Tea A. Calais 20.30 D. Calais 21.20 A. Bethune 23.00 Supper Bs.	D. Bethune 08.45 A. Beaucourt 09.55 Lunch & D. Beaucourt 16.58 Tea A. Bethune 18.15	D. Bethune 10.00 A. Vimy 10.30 Lunch & D. Vimy 16.16 Tea A. Bethune 16.45	D. Bethune 07.15 A. Ypres 09.14	Ecole Payante. Breakfast. Lunch. Tea.	12.52	15.59
N WOMEN'S SECTION II (2nd Class)	(From West and N West)	D. Dover 17.15 Lunch Tn D. Dover 19.15 Tea A. Calais 20.30 D. Calais 21.30 A. Hazebrouck 22.30 Supper Bs.	D. Hazebrouck 09.00 A. Vimy 10.10 Lunch & D. Vimy 17.05 Tea A. Hazebrouck 18.25	D. Hazebrouck 09.00 A. Beaucourt 09.55 Lunch & D. Beaucourt 16.30 Tea A. Hazebrouck 18.35	D. Hazebrouck 08.45 A. Ypres 09.44	Ecole Payante. Breakfast. Lunch Tea.	12.56	16.45
O SCOTTISH	D. Scotland Lunch D. Tilbury 23.59 Supper Tn.	A. Dunkirk 06.45 Breakfast A. Dunkirk 08.05 A. Cambrai 11.00 Lunch Bs	D. Cambrai 09.15 A. Beaucourt 10.40 Lunch & D. Beaucourt 17.15 Tea A. Cambrai 18.45	D. Cambrai 10.08 A. Vimy 11.20 Lunch & D. Vimy 17.15 Tea A. Cambrai 18.20	D. Cambrai 07.00 A. Ypres 09.57	Caserne Inf. Breakfast. Lunch Tea.	13.12	17.30
P WEST MIDLAND II. & EAST MIDLAND II.	Supper Tn D. Tilbury 23.59	A. Dunkirk 06.45 Breakfast D. Dunkirk 08.25 A. Valenciennes 11.30 Lunch Bs	D. Valenciennes 09.40 A. Beaucourt 11.30 Lunch & D. Beaucourt 18.00 Tea A. Valenciennes 19.45	D. Valenciennes 09.40 A. Vimy 11.05 Lunch & D. Vimy 17.35 Tea A. Valenciennes 18.55	D. Valenciennes 08.10 A. Ypres 10.15	Convent de la St. Famille. Lunch. Tea.	14.08	17.45
Q NORTH-WESTERN I.		Tea and D. Tilbury 23.59 Supper Tn	D. Dunkirk 06.45 Breakfast D. Dunkirk 08.20 A. Lille 10.35 Lunch Ba.	D. Lille 10.00 A. Beaucourt 11.40 Lunch & D. Beaucourt 16.58 Tea A. Lille 18.30	D. Lille 06.20 A. Ypres 01.33	Prison. Breakfast. Lunch. Tea.	13.28	16.35
R NORTH-WESTERN II.		Tea and D. Tilbury 23.59 Supper Tn	D. Dunkirk 06.45 Breakfast D. Dunkirk 08.15 A. Lille 10.15 Lunch Bs.	D. Lille 10.35 A. Beaucourt 12.10 Lunch & D. Beaucourt 17.35 Tea A. Lille 19.16	D. Lille 06.00 A. Ypres 07.14	Prison. Breakfast. Lunch Tea.	13.24	16.30
S EAST ANGLIA	D. Harwich 23.00 Tea	Breakfast A. Zeebrugge 07.00 Steamer D. Zeebrugge 11.10 A. Armentieres 13.50 Lunch Bs.	D. Armentieres 09.40 A. Beaucourt 11.50 Lunch & D. Beaucourt 17.30 Tea A. Armentieres 19.15	D. Armentieres 09.25 A. Vimy 10.38 Lunch & D. Vimy 16.25 Tea A. Armentieres 17.10	D. Armentieres 07.00 A. Ypres 08.15	Ecole Moyen. Breakfast. Lunch Tea.	13.52	18.20
T¹ YORKSHIRE		D. Yorkshire Supper Tn. D. Harwich 23.00 Tea	Breakfast A. Zeebrugge 07.00 Steamer A. Zeebrugge 11.10 A. Ypres 13.30 Lunch Ba	D. Ypres 07.15 A. Beaucourt 10.50 Lunch & D. Beaucourt 16.20 Tea A. Ypres 19.40	At Ypres	Abattoir. Lunch Tea.	13.40	At Y...
T² YORKSHIRE		D. Yorkshire Supper Tn. D. Harwich 23.00 Tea	Breakfast A. Zeebrugge 07.00 Steamer D. Zeebrugge 11.10 A. Poperinghe 13.20 Lunch Bs.	D. Poperinghe 07.35 A. Beaucourt 10.50 Lunch & D. Beaucourt 16.20 Tea A. Poperinghe 19.21		Abattoir. Lunch Tea.	13.40	(Motor to & fro...)

	AUGUST 9TH.		AUGUST 10TH.		Meals, etc., required in Billets.	
als.		Meals.		Meals.		
	D. Calais 01.00 A. Dover 02.30 Tea D. Dover 04.00 A. London 06.08				Bed & Breakfast Aug. 4/5th. Supper, Bed & Breakfast Aug. 5/6th. 6/7th. 7/9th.	A
per	D. Dover 02.00 A. London 04.25				Bed & Breakfast Aug. 4/5th. Supper, Bed & Breakfast Aug. 5/6th. 6/7th. 7/9th.	B
per	Via Reading				Lunch, Aug. 5th. Supper, Bed & Breakfast Aug. 5/6th. 6/7th. 7/9th.	C
per	Via Guildford				Lunch, Aug. 5th. Supper, Bed & Breakfast Aug. 5/6th. 6/7th. 7/9th.	D
per	A. Dover 01.00 Tea D. Dover 02.30 A. Kensington 05.05				Lunch, Aug. 5th. Supper, Bed & Breakfast Aug. 5/6th. 6/7th. 7/9th.	E
per	A. Dover 01.00 Tea D. Dover 03.00 A. London 05.25				Lunch, Aug. 5th. Supper, Bed & Breakfast Aug. 5/6th. 6/7th. 7/9th.	F
	D. Calais 01.00 A. Dover 02.30 Tea D. Dover 04.15 A. London 06.32				Supper, Bed & Breakfast Aug. 5/6th. 6/7th. 7/9th. Lunch. Aug. 5th.	G
	D. Lens 07.00 A. Boulogne 10.15 D. Boulogne 10.30 D. Dover 12.00 Lunch D. Dover 13.45 Supper Tn. A. London 16.01				Supper, Bed & Breakfast Aug. 5/6th. 6/7th. 7/8th. 8/9th. Tea. Aug 5th.	H
per	A. Kensington 02.25				Supper, Bed & Breakfast Aug. 5/6th. 6/7th. 7/9th. Meat Tea. Aug 5th.	I
per	*D. Dover 02.15 A. London 04.45				Supper, Bed & Breakfast Aug. 5/6th. 6/7th. 7/8th.	J
	D. Arras 07.50 D. Boulogne 10.35 Lunch D. Boulogne 18.30 Tea D. Dover 20.00 D. Dover 22.00 Supper Tn. 22.15	A. Kensington 00.15 00.30		Bed & Breakfast Aug. 5/6th. Bed & Breakfast 6/7th. 7/8th. 8/9th.	K
	D. Roubaix 07.15 A. Boulogne 10.00 D. Boulogne 10.30 A. Dover 12.00 Lunch D. Dover 13.45 A. London 15.29				Supper, Bed & Breakfast Aug. 5/6th. 6/7th. 7/8th. 8/9th.	L
	D. Bethune 09.00 A. Calais 10.25 Lunch A. Calais 17.00 Tea D. Dover 18.30 Supper D. Dover 20.00				Supper, Bed & Breakfast Aug. 5/6th. 6/7th. 7/8th. 8/9th.	M 2nd Class
	D. Hazebrouck 09.45 A. Calais 10.45 Lunch A. Calais 17.00 Tea A. Dover 18.30 Supper B. Dover 20.15	A. London 22.14 (9th Aug.)		Supper, Bed & Breakfast Aug. 5/6th. 6/7th. 7/8th. 8/9th.	N 2nd Class
	Via Reading				Supper, Bed & Breakfast Aug. 5/6th. 6/7th. 7/8th. 8/9th.	O 2nd Class
per	A. Tilbury 05.30 Bkfast Tn. D. Tilbury 06.30 Lunch Tn. A. Scotland Tea Tn.				Supper, Bed & Breakfast Aug. 5/6th. 6/7th. 7/8th. Lunch. Aug. 5th.	P
per	A. Tilbury 05.30 Bkfast Tn.				Supper, Bed & Breakfast Aug. 5/6th. 6/7th. 7/8th. Lunch. Aug. 5th.	Q
	D. Lille 09.40 A. Vimy 10.46 Lunch & D. Vimy 17.15 Tea A. Dunkirk 19.25 D. Dunkirk 21.30 Supper	A. Tilbury 05.00 Bkfast Tn.		Supper, Bed & Breakfast Aug. 6/7th. 7/8th. 8/9th. Lunch. Aug. 6th.	R
	D. Lille 09.45 A. Vimy 10.55 Lunch & D. Vimy 17.35 Tea A. Dunkirk 19.40 Supper D. Dunkirk 21.30	A. Tilbury 05.00 Breakfast Lunch Tn.		Supper, Bed & Breakfast Aug. 6/7th. 7/8th. 8/9th. Lunch. Aug. 6th.	S
Supper Steamer	A. Harwich 05.00 Breakfast Steamer				Supper, Bed & Breakfast Aug. 5/6th. 6/7th. 7/8th. Lunch. Aug. 5th.	
	D. Ypres 08.25 A. Vimy 10.35 Lunch & D. Vimy 16.45 Tea A. Zeebrugge 21.00 D. Zeebrugge 22.00 Supper	A. Harwich 05.00 Breakfast Lunch Tn.		Supper, Bed & Breakfast Aug. 6/7th. 7/8th. 8/9th. Lunch. Aug. 6th.	T'
	D. Poperinghe 08.38 A. Vimy 10.35 Lunch D. Vimy 16.45 Tea A. Zeebrugge 21.00 D. Zeebrugge 22.00 Supper Steamer	A. Harwich 05.00 Breakfast Steamer or Lunch Tn.		Supper, Bed & Breakfast Aug. 6/7th. 7/8th. 8/9th. Lunch. Aug. 6th.	T''

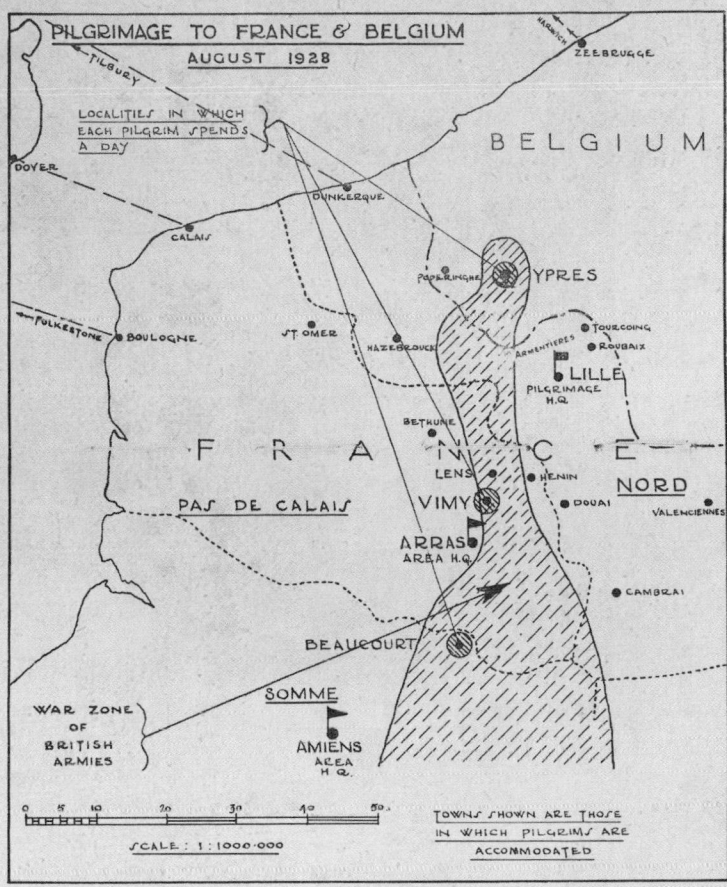

PILGRIMAGE TO FRANCE & BELGIUM
AUGUST 1928

LOCALITIES IN WHICH EACH PILGRIM SPENDS A DAY

BELGIUM

FRANCE NORD

PAS DE CALAIS

WAR ZONE OF BRITISH ARMIES

SOMME

SCALE : 1 : 1000·000

TOWNS SHOWN ARE THOSE IN WHICH PILGRIMS ARE ACCOMMODATED

ABOVE Pilgrims all got the chance to visit the Somme and Arras sectors before converging on Ypres.

LEFT To coordinate the movements of 11,000 pilgrims, a complicated railway schedule was devised.

ABOVE Amassed female
pilgrims awaiting their
departure from
Victoria station.

Special trains were laid on, and some railway workers put in eighteen-hour days to get the travellers to their boats on time. The majority went from Dover, with the Southern Railway agreeing to carry an additional 7,500 passengers in a single 24-hour period, despite being already busy with summer-holiday traffic. Others were sent by rail to Tilbury and Harwich. Of course, this wasn't wartime, and several thousand civilians could not be expected to put up with the privations the BEF might have endured, so the organizers had the extra headache of needing to factor in breaks for refreshments en route.

Tickets for the pilgrimage cost just £4 5s, covering travel from London, accommodation and meals. This low price was made possible in part by the railway companies, who agreed to offer reduced fares. But it was also dependent on the hospitality of local people in France and Belgium, many of whom provided billets for pilgrims for a modest fee – while other visitors were accommodated in public venues such as schools and colleges.

To prepare the pilgrims for their Continental adventure, they were each given a book setting out the order of events and packed with helpful information. It told them what to wear – sensible shoes were a must for traversing cobbled streets; what to pack – 'not more than you can comfortably carry for a mile, and do not forget to take a waterproof'; and even warned them not to expect their French and Belgian hosts to cater to every British taste: 'It should be noted that tea will probably not be a feature of the . . . menu, coffee being the national equivalent.'

Indeed, food and drink was a major headache for the trip's organizers. The pilgrims' morning and evening meals were provided in their billets, but during the day each trainload of pilgrims followed its own three-day programme, which included prearranged visits to the Somme battlefields and Vimy Ridge, where a carefully reconstructed trench system could be explored – the guidebook presciently noting that 'no doubt, for generations to come, it will be visited by our descendants when they wish to study the old-fashioned methods of fighting that were employed in the Great War of 1914–18'.

ABOVE AND RIGHT
Pilgrims from all over Britain joined the journey of remembrance.

This busy itinerary meant that lunch and other refreshments had to be provided on the hoof. The Legion called on the Parisian company Messrs Félix Potin, described in a souvenir book published after the pilgrimage as 'the French Lyons', to make up packed lunches for the crowds. Sixteen railway trucks per day carried food and drink between Paris and the pilgrimage sites, including 23,500 slices of ham, 26,500 bananas and 31,500 bottles of mineral water and beer. Since it was apparently 'inconceivable that tea should be excluded from the Pilgrims' daily menu', this was the chance to offer a cup to the parched travellers, and field kitchens set up on the battlefields brewed up 26,000 quarts of Britain's favourite beverage over the course of the trip.

The climax of the three-day event was a ceremony in Ypres. As the gateway to the Channel ports, the city had been of vital strategic importance during the war, and British troops had succeeded in holding it for the four long years of fighting. It witnessed five major battles, and hundreds of thousands of British troops had met their deaths in the surrounding area, with the city itself being almost completely destroyed. By 1928, reconstruction was under way, though the iconic medieval Cloth Hall would not be completely rebuilt until the 1960s.

A recent addition to the still-ravaged landscape was the British-built Menin Gate, designed by Sir Reginald Blomfield and unveiled in

LEFT Pilgrims at the ruins of the Cloth Hall in Ypres.

RIGHT Sir Reginald Blomfield's Menin Gate in Ypres – the first 'Memorial to the Missing'.

BELOW Ex-servicemen with their wreaths for the ceremony at the Menin Gate.

LEFT Michael Portillo pays homage to the fallen at the Menin Gate in Ypres.

1927. Built on a causeway over the city's medieval moat, it marked the point where thousands of British servicemen had marched out of Ypres towards the trenches, many of whom never returned. Engraved with the names of more than 54,000 servicemen, it was also the first of the Western Front's 'Memorials to the Missing', which commemorated the thousands of soldiers without any known grave. It was here that the pilgrims would gather for a Ceremony of Remembrance.

Early in the morning of 8 August 1928, the first of the trains pulled into Ypres station and organizers began the daunting task of overseeing the arrival and distribution of 11,000 pilgrims around the city to prearranged assembly points. There, the pilgrims were given breakfast and the chance to freshen up before the official proceedings began. As they waited, perhaps some heeded the advice of their guidebooks, which suggested: 'At such periods it may be that Community Songs will help to pass the time of waiting and to weld the Pilgrimage into one great host' – obligingly providing the words to a variety of songs ranging from 'Pack Up Your Troubles' to 'Land Of Hope And Glory', 'in order to assist the memory'.

At eleven o'clock sharp, every pilgrim was in position and the Menin Gate ceremony, broadcast live by the BBC, began. After it, the pilgrims processed under the arch of the gate and on into the town, saluting the Prince of Wales, who stood on a dais outside the Cloth Hall. As the photographs attest, the marching hordes made for an extraordinary sight. For those who had known Ypres in its darkest days, it must have been a day of mixed emotions. As one pilgrim later recalled:

> I couldn't help thinking of the days when you had to cross this same place on your hands and knees, darting to cover as best you could, with shells dropping continually, when Ypres was surely worse than Hell itself. What a change that day with the bands playing, flags flying and all the houses rebuilt. I could see in my mind's eye the phantom army that had marched that way, never to return.

The railways had played their part in an unforgettable event. Afterwards, the British Legion published A Souvenir of the Battlefields Pilgrimage, so that pilgrims could relive the extraordinary experience and those who had not been able to join the crowds could share in its spirit:

THE PILGRIM'S HOMAGE

LEFT All 11,000 pilgrims passed through the Menin Gate in an extraordinary tribute to those lost in the First World War.

The pilgrims journeyed to the Battlefields of France and Flanders, not in uniform nor holiday garb, but in the mufti of their everyday life, not to raise the paean of victory, not to stage a triumph but to show to the world that their loved ones are not forgotten and, above all, that the purpose for which they died is still remembered.

Prince and ploughman, general and private soldier, mother and widow, found unity in something greater even than the discipline of war, and, on the very scenes of their kinsmen's sacrifice, renewed afresh their consecration to the ideal for which it was made.

BRITAIN'S RAILWAYS AFTER THE ARMISTICE – THE BEGINNING OF THE END OF THE LINE?

In 1913, record numbers of British tourists had crossed the Channel to embark on Continental railway adventures. Then, the outbreak of war brought such pleasure-seeking to an abrupt halt. For four years, hundreds of thousands of young men traced the same route, but their travelling clothes were replaced by uniforms, their suitcases by kitbags. They were bound not for comfortable hotels but cold, sodden trenches, haunted by the ghosts of their fallen comrades. By the time of the British Legion's Epic Pilgrimage in 1928, on the surface things had come full circle for the railways. The tourist trade was back in business, and the trains had finally swapped deadly cargoes of munitions for the fruits of peacetime commerce. But the mourning pilgrims wending their way to the devastated city of Ypres cut very different figures from the happy-go-lucky tourists of the Belle Epoque.

The experience of war had scarred a generation. Servicemen had seen sights they would never forget. Millions had sustained life-changing injuries. Whole communities had been decimated by the disappearance of sons, brothers, fiancés and friends. And the war's after-effects reached beyond the personal. In its wake, empires had crumbled. With the abdication of the German Kaiser Wilhelm II and the renunciation of constitutional powers by Austrian Emperor Charles I, two of Europe's most powerful dynasties lost their centuries-long grip on the Continent. The Ottoman Empire was carved up, ending 500 years of dominance over the Near East. Meanwhile, in Russia, the conflict had seen the overthrow of Tsar Nicholas II and the Bolshevik revolution. The British Empire lived on, but weakened and ripe for the further changes the century would bring.

Britain's proud railway industry had not escaped this tidal wave of change. Throughout the Railway Age of the nineteenth century, the groundbreaking technology of steam and tracks had helped Britain prosper. Built on rail power, the workshop of the world used the tracks to deliver its exports across the globe. Now, as Britain adjusted to the new order of the post-war era, the first signs of the railways' slow twentieth-century decline were beginning to show. The conflict had stimulated and accelerated the development of rival forms of transport that would

ultimately overtake the railways. Although it would still be some time before either air travel or the roads posed a serious threat, the first scheduled international commercial flight took off from London for Paris in 1919, and as ex-army lorries flooded the market after the armistice, small haulage firms began to challenge the railways' dominance over freight.

In the short term, Britain's railways had more pressing problems to deal with. Under government control for the duration of the conflict, the railway companies had carried out millions of pounds' worth of war work, from transporting troops to manufacturing munitions. They had sent men and rolling stock to France and Belgium, and even torn up their tracks to supply the front line with the railway material it desperately needed. The war had imposed hidden costs too, as essential investment and maintenance of tracks and trains were deferred. According to the *Railway Gazette*:

> *By the end of August, 1918, the companies were short of about 2,000 new locomotives and about 33,000 wagons which, under normal conditions, they would have built since the beginning of*

ABOVE The first scheduled international flight – a single-engined De Havilland DH4A G-EAJC flies from London to Paris, 25 August 1919.

RIGHT Railwaymen picketing a station during the 1919 strike.

the war. In addition to this there were awaiting repair, at the same date, 5,000 locomotives, or more than one-fifth of the total stock owned by the companies.

What was more, the railways were soon facing high prices for essential materials and a dramatically increased wage bill. Having worked punishing hours throughout the war, in early 1919 rail workers won the right to an eight-hour day. And after a dispute that culminated in a national railway strike in the autumn of that year, they had also succeeded in securing significant pay rises. Within three years of the armistice, the industry was losing well over £20 million a year.

Clearly, the railways' finances needed urgent attention. Before the conflict, it had been agreed that the companies would be compensated for any losses sustained while under state control. Now, the detail of how much would be paid had to be worked out and agreed. To balance the books, the railways also needed to find ways to boost revenues fast. And while these issues were being debated, there were bigger questions to answer about the future of the industry.

The experience of conflict had demonstrated the power of centralization. Agents of the state, from the Ministry of Munitions to transport tsar Sir Eric Geddes, had achieved extraordinary feats as part of a formidable war machine. Central control of Britain's railways had produced impressive efficiency savings. For example, before the war, a perennial problem was the returning of empty wagons to their proprietary company, which clogged up the network. During wartime, all wagons had been pooled, enabling the authorities to slash the number of unproductive journeys.

LEFT Lloyd George, who became Prime Minister in December 1916.

Now, as the nation attempted to rise from the ashes, some believed that the state should continue to play a bigger role in people's lives. The Ministry for Reconstruction had been set up in 1917 to oversee the transition to peacetime, and dreamed up schemes for unprecedented social intervention, including the building of hundreds of thousands of new homes 'fit for heroes'. And Britain's railways, born when Victorian-era laissez-faire was at its height, were now in the reformers' sights.

Just a month after the armistice, Lloyd George (who had become Prime Minister in December 1916 and whose mandate was renewed in the general election of December 1918 – the first to count the votes of women over 30) issued a policy statement, later reproduced by Edwin Pratt:

> *Some of the ablest transportation advisers of the Government have already got plans. The war has shown how much could be effected in the way of rapid development of our transportation system behind the lines, especially by laying down hundreds, if not thousands, of miles of light railways. If this were done in this country, especially*

in connection with an improvement of our roads, it would achieve
great results in the opening up of the resources of the country and
the spreading of the population into healthier areas.

Could a Geddes-style transport revolution benefit Britain in peacetime? And how could such a transformation be effected? Should nationalization be considered? Or was that a step too far? To buy time for these questions to be answered, in 1919 an Act of Parliament extended government control of the network for a further two years. In place of the wartime Railway Executive Committee, the railways would now be run by a new Ministry for Transport – headed, as we have seen, by Sir Eric Geddes himself. The new department would oversee the railways' contribution to demobilization and reconstruction, whilst also formulating a plan for their future.

As the Whitehall mandarins got to work, measures were put in place to try to stabilize the railways' finances. On the recommendation of a newly formed Rates Advisory Committee, passengers and freight customers faced big price hikes. In 1920, passenger fares were raised by a whopping 75 per cent compared to pre-war prices, season tickets by 50 per cent, and 'workmen's fares' – affordable tickets that the railways had been obliged to provide since the Cheap Trains Act of 1883 – were effectively abolished. Unsurprisingly, this was not popular with passengers, especially as the new fares took effect in August, the height of the holiday season. Travelling on uncomfortable, run-down and now much more expensive trains, people were losing patience with the railways, and when it came to the issue of compensation public opinion was not on the companies' side.

While a committee tried to establish how much was owed, the press reported that the industry was claiming huge sums of up to £400 million, creating the impression that the railways were greedy and perhaps even trying to profit from the war. This was strenuously denied by the railway companies, and indeed the committee concluded that the highest potential claim was £150 million. In the end, after negotiations with the ministry, the industry accepted just £60 million in compensation. And this disappointing payout coincided with the announcement of a radical restructuring of Britain's railways.

The Railways Act of 1921 stopped short of nationalization but still swept away the multiplicity of 178 independent, competing firms that had evolved out of the dizzy years of railway mania. Under its terms, these erstwhile rivals were required to merge into just four big regional concerns. Each had a foothold in London, then controlled its own quadrant of the country, roughly split into east- and north-east England and eastern Scotland; the Midlands, north-west England and western Scotland; southern England; and the West Country and Wales. The original aim of the scheme had been to eliminate competition as far as possible, but, after protests from the British Chamber of Commerce among others, some competing routes survived, with, for example, the western and southern groups both running services through Devon and Cornwall to Plymouth.

Henceforth, fares would be regulated by a government-appointed Railway Rates Tribunal, which would aim to maintain the companies' profits at pre-war levels. Likewise, a Central Wages Board would arbitrate in the case of wage disputes between workers and bosses. Many of the railway managers viewed this as a narrow escape, since the original white paper had proposed that workers should sit alongside shareholder representatives on the boards of the reconfigured railway companies – a suggestion that was met with horror. The act's critics called it 'a hotchpotch of Communism and individualism', while its defenders saw it as the perfect compromise, retaining the efficiencies of scale the war era had demonstrated while maintaining some of the virtues of competition. But whatever its advantages and disadvantages, it showed, in the words of Edwin Pratt, 'a complete reversal . . . in the traditional policy of the State towards the railways'. We have been debating the best way to balance private and public control of the railways ever since.

The age of the 'Big Four', as the grouped companies became known, proved short-lived. Constrained by new regulations and facing ever-increasing rivalry from the roads, by 1939 Britain's railways had failed to recover anything like their pre-war power and profitability. Indeed, according to Christian Wolmar, by the eve of World War Two only one of the companies was paying out a dividend.

The Second World War was not a railway war in the same way as the First had been. On the battlefield, newer technologies dominated, and the conflict was much more mobile than its predecessor. Nevertheless, railways were still a vital link in the supply chain, and on the home front in Britain they endured extraordinary overuse as petrol rationing forced

RIGHT A joint advertisement by the London Midland and Scottish (LMS) and London and North Eastern (LNER) – two of the new railway companies to emerge after the Railways Act of 1921 was passed.

THE CLYDE
VIEW APPROACHING BRODICK - ISLE OF ARRAN
by Norman Wilkinson, P.R.I.

LMS

LNER

IT'S QUICKER BY RAIL

FULL INFORMATION FROM ANY LMS or L·N·E·R STATION or AGENCY

road users back onto the rails. Once again, the network was seized by the government for the duration of the conflict, and by the time it was over Britain's broken railways were a shadow of their former selves. This time, with the election of the Labour government in the immediate aftermath of the war, all-out nationalization was inevitable. The creation of British Railways marked the final end of the private companies that – though much changed – could trace their roots back to the dawn of the Railway Age. Arguably, the First World War had been the first step on the road to this railway revolution.

LESSONS OF THE RAILWAY WAR

The railway history of the First World War is, of course, just one part of the story. But viewing the war through the lens of the railways allows us to glimpse unseen aspects of this terrible conflict. It reveals that victory depended on logistics just as much as on military might. From the conception of the Schlieffen Plan onwards, railways were acknowledged as the key to supplying a twentieth-century force in the field. The available railway resources helped shape military outcomes – from the Race to the Sea, which created the Western Front, through the Allies' 1916 transport crisis, right up to the failure of the German spring offensive in 1918.

We cannot fail to be impressed by some of the phenomenal achievements of the railway war. Ambulance trains saved countless lives and offered the wounded quick access to sophisticated treatments. The supply chain that kept millions fed on the Western Front was awe-inspiring in its efficiency. The railway troops of the Royal Engineers built new lines at almost unimaginable speed in hostile conditions. And the 1916 transport revolution in France, spearheaded by the dynamic railway manager Sir Eric Geddes, provides a counterpoint to the view that Britain's leaders were ineffectual and out of touch with the real war taking place in the trenches.

But the dynamism injected by the railways gave rise to a paradox. The technology that facilitated the rapid projection of military might across vast distances in a matter of hours simultaneously served as the conflict's ball and chain. The railways carried vast quantities of men and materiel to the front line with dazzling efficiency – but only as far as the railheads. For either side to advance, the attacking force, weighed down by these cumbersome trappings of twentieth-century war, had to leave the tracks behind, cutting themselves off from their supply chain, while the defending side could use the rails to bring in reinforcements, strengthening their ability to repel the attack. By favouring the defensive, railway-age technology perpetuated the stalemate. For both sides, the tracks became the trammels that imprisoned them in their dugouts, feeding a seemingly interminable war of attrition.

For railway fans it is hard to stomach the fact that magnificent steam locomotives transported so many to their deaths. But this was just one of many ways in which the First World War warped symbols of progress, transforming them into instruments of death. The image of a cutting-edge petrol locomotive hauling munitions through a shell-torn landscape eloquently expresses how the inventiveness of the industrial age was harnessed to destruction.

On the home front, tracing the war's effects on Britain's railways demonstrates in microcosm the far-reaching impact of total war. The nation's patriotic response to the conflict is evident in the industry's rush to lend its rich resources to the war effort. Men, workshops and ships; land for allotments and station buffets for soldiers – all were offered up for King and country. But faced with unprecedented demands on its services, state control and the loss of huge numbers of workers, the powerful, self-confident, male-dominated industry of Edwardian times was forced to reinvent itself, never again to return to its pre-war form.

The personal war stories of railwaymen bring to life the human cost of the conflict. By picturing their pre-war routines in the familiar ordered world of the Edwardian railway we can start to imagine just how disconcerting the shift to the chaos of conflict must have been. Indeed, for many servicemen the railways were the bridge between the alien world of the Western Front and the altered but still essentially familiar surroundings of civilian life back in 'Blighty'. As they travelled by train between these two spheres, the journey must have felt like a kind of no-man's-land of its own.

But railways also offered shared experiences. Letters, parcels and leave brought civilians and soldiers into contact. Tearful farewells, emotional reunions and solemn remembrance – all were accompanied by the taste and smells of soot and steam, by the rumble of locomotive engines and the shrill shriek of the whistle. The railways were the backdrop to the everyday experience of war, and today perhaps they can serve to connect us to this chapter in our history. As we travel the same tracks and pass through the same stations – still dominated by war memorials – we can try to enter into the mindset of those who lived through the dark days of the First World War.

RIGHT The First
World War saw
the railways – an
emblem of civilized
progress – turned
to destructive ends.
The price was paid
by millions of young
men, transported by
rail to the battlefields.
For many it was a
one-way journey.

PICTURE CREDITS

BIBLIOGRAPHY

Throughout the book I have tried to indicate the main sources for each story within the text. What follows is a more comprehensive, but not exhaustive, list of references. The works listed under 'General' have all been used extensively throughout. Then more specific sources are listed by chapter under their story subheading. For simplicity, each source is listed only once, under the story for which it was primarily used, though it may also have been referred to elsewhere. Responsibility for any inadvertent omissions is my own.

GENERAL

Pratt, Edwin, *British Railways and the Great War* (London: Selwyn & Blount, 1921). The two volumes are available at http://archive.org/details/cu31924092566128 and http://archive.org/details/cu31924092566136

Railway Gazette: Special War Transportation Number (Stockport: The Moseley Railway Trust, 2013 [first edition by the *Railway Gazette*, 1920]).

Stevenson, David, *With Our Backs to the Wall: Victory and Defeat in 1918* (London: Allen Lane, 2011).

Stevenson, David, *1914–1918: The History of the First World War* (London: Penguin, 2012).

Westwood, J. N., *Railways at War* (London: Osprey Publishing Company, 1980).

Wolmar, Christian, *Fire and Steam: How the Railways Transformed Britain* (London: Atlantic, 2007, Kindle edition).

Wolmar, Christian, *Engines of War: How Wars Were Won and Lost on the Railways* (London: Atlantic Books, 2012).

WEB RESOURCES

British Library World War One resources http://www.bl.uk/world-war-one

Imperial War Museum podcasts http://www.1914.org/category/podcasts/

For information on the British Army www.1914-1918.net

INTRODUCTION

Bradshaw's Continental Railway Guide (Oxford: Old House Books & Maps, 2012).

Emmerson, Charles, *1913: The World Before the Great War* (London: The Bodley Head, 2013).

More, Charles, *The Industrial Age: Economy and Society in Britain, 1750–1995* (London: Longman, 1997).

Nock, O. S., *World Atlas of Railways* (London: Mitchell Beazley, 1978).

Porter, Andrew (ed.), *The Oxford History of the British Empire: Volume III: The Nineteenth Century* (Oxford: Oxford University Press, 1999).

CHAPTER 1 – A RAILWAY WAR BEGINS

Europe's Railway Plans are Born

Hobsbawm, Eric, *Age of Empire 1875–1914* (London: Weidenfeld & Nicolson, 2010, Kindle edition).

Railway Manual: War (Uckfield, Naval & Military Press, 2009 [London: HMSO, 1911]).

Stevenson David, 'War by Timetable? The Railway Race before 1914', *Past & Present,* No. 162 (February 1999).

Van Creveld, Martin, *Supplying War: Logistics from Wallenstein to Patton* (Cambridge: Cambridge University Press, 2004).

War by Timetable – The Climax to the Railway Age?

Taylor, A. J. P., *The First World War: An Illustrated History* (London: Penguin, 1966).

Taylor, A. J. P., *War by Timetable: How the First World War Began* (Endeavour Press, 2013, Kindle edition).

A False Start to the Railway War

Heal, David, *Victims Nonetheless: The Invasion of Luxembourg, 1914* (Luxembourg, 2013, Kindle edition).

Thewes, Guy, *Les gouvernements du Grand-Duché de Luxembourg depuis 1848* (Luxembourg: Service information et presse, 2011). In French. Available to download from http://www.luxembourg.public.lu/en/publications/politics/index.html

Mobilization – The British Expeditionary Force Takes to the Tracks

Downham, Peter (ed.), *The Diary of an Old Contemptible: From Mons to Baghdad 1914–1919* (Barnsley: Pen and Sword Books, 2004, Kindle edition).

Jeffery, Keith, *Field Marshal Sir Henry Wilson: A Political Soldier* (Oxford: Oxford University Press, 2006).

Battle of the Marne – Railways and the War of Movement

Beckett, Ian, *Ypres: The First Battle 1914* (Abingdon: Routledge, 2013).

Senior, Ian, *Home Before the Leaves Fall: A New History of the German Invasion of 1914* (Oxford: Osprey, 2012).

Tuchman, Barbara, *The Guns of August* (London: Constable & Robinson Ltd, 2000).

CHAPTER 2 – RISING TO THE CHALLENGE

Answering the Call – The North Eastern Railway Pals

Langham, Rob, *The North Eastern Railway in the First World War* (Stroud: Fonthill Media, 2013).

Shakespear, J., *A Record of the 17th and 32nd Battalions Northumberland Fusiliers, 1914–1919* (Newcastle upon Tyne: Northumberland Press Ltd, 1926).

Ambulance Trains

Anonymous, *Diary of a Nursing Sister on the Western Front, 1914–1915* (Edinburgh and London: William Blackwood and Sons, 1915), as seen at http://www.gutenberg.org/files/18910/18910-h/18910-h.htm

The Main Supply – Manufacturing and Moving Munitions

Darroch, G. R. S., *Deeds of a Great Railway: A Record of the Enterprise and Achievements of the London & North-Western Railway Company during the Great War* (London: John Murray, 1920).

Marwick, Arthur, *Women at War 1914–18* (Glasgow: Fontana Original, 1977).

Thom, Deborah, *Nice Girls and Rude Girls: Women Workers in World War I* (London: I. B. Tauris & Co., 1998).

The Railway Branch of the Royal Engineers

History of the Corps of Royal Engineers: Vol. V: The Home Front, France, Flanders and Italy in the First World War (Chatham: The Institution of Royal Engineers, 1951).

Ronald, D. W. and Carter, R. J., *The Longmoor Military Railway* (Newton Abbot: David & Charles, 1974).

Ronald, Colonel David and Christensen, Mike OBE, *The Longmoor Military Railway: A New History, Volume One: 1903–1939* (Lydney: Lightmoor Press, 2012).

Railway Guns

Clarke, Dale, *British Artillery 1914–19: Heavy Artillery* (Oxford: Osprey, 2010, Kindle edition).

http://www.disused stations.org.uk/features/index6.shtml

CHAPTER 3 – KEEPING THE WAR MOVING

Sir Eric Geddes – Forgotten Hero of the Railway War

Brown, Ian Malcolm, *British Logistics on the Western Front: 1914–1919* (Westport, Connecticut: Praeger, 1998).

Grieves, Keith, *Sir Eric Geddes: Business and Government in War and Peace* (Manchester: Manchester University Press, 1989).

Grieves, Keith, 'Geddes, Sir Eric Campbell (1875–1937)', *Oxford Dictionary of National Biography* (Oxford: Oxford University Press, 2004); online edition, January 2011, http://www.oxforddnb.com/view/article/33360, accessed 5 Feb 2014.

Light Railways – Changing the Way the War Moved

Davies, W. J. K., *Light Railways of the First World War: A History of Tactical Rail Communications on the British Fronts, 1914–18* (Newton Abbot: David & Charles, 1967).

Leonard, Matt, 'The Foundations of the Battle of Arras', http://ww1centenary. oucs.ox.ac.uk/?p=593, by license as Creative Commons Attribution-Non-Commercial-Share Alike 2.0 UK: England & Wales (http:// creativecommons.org/licenses/by-nc-sa/2.0/uk/).

Taylorson, Keith, *Narrow Gauge at War* (Croydon: Plateway Press, 1987).

Feeding Morale – Food Supply on the Front and at Home

Brophy, J. and Partridge, E., *The Long Trail: Soldiers' Songs and Slang 1914–18* (London: Sphere Books, 1969).

Duffet, Rachel, 'The Stomach for Fighting: Food on the Western Front', BBC Essex website, http:// www.bbc.co.uk/essex/content/ articles/2008/11/04/food_western_ front_feature.shtml

Grant, Peter, *Philanthropy and Voluntary Action in the First World War: Mobilizing Charity* (Abingdon: Routledge, 2014).

Henniker, A. M., *Transportation on the Western Front 1914–1918* (London: HMSO, 1937).

Ward, Chris, *Living on the Western Front: Annals and Stories* (London: Bloomsbury, 2013).

The Bath Railway Poet

Chappell, Henry, *The Day and Other Poems* (London: John Lane, The Bodley Head, 1918).

http://www.bl.uk/world-war-one/ articles/atrocity-propaganda

Station Canteens

Gittins, Sandra, *The Great Western Railway in the First World War* (Stroud: The History Press, 2010).

Quintinshill – The Worst Railway Disaster in British History

Hamilton, J. A. B., *Britain's Greatest Rail Disaster: The Quintinshill Blaze of 1915* (London: George Allen and Unwin Ltd, 1969).

Richards, Jack and Searle, Adrian, *The Quintinshill Conspiracy: The Shocking True Story Behind Britain's Worst Rail Disaster* (Barnsley: Pen & Sword, 2013).

Thomas, John, *Gretna: Britain's Worst Railway Disaster (1915)* (Newton Abbot: David & Charles, 1969).

CHAPTER 4 – ON TRACK TO VICTORY

Women on the Rails

Gregory, Adrian, 'Railway Stations: Gateways and Termini', in *Capital Cities at War*, Vol II, Jay Winter and Jean-Louis Robert (eds) (Cambridge: Cambridge University Press, 2007).

Matheson, Rosa, *The Fairer Sex: Women and the Great Western Railway* (Stroud: Tempus, 2007).

Wojtczak, Helena, *Railwaywomen* (Hastings: The Hastings Press, 2005).

http://historywardrobe.wordpress. com/2014/02/05/railway-women-in-ww1/

London Lines

Bosanquet, Nick, *Our Land at War,* (Stroud: The History Press, 2014).

Wolmar, Christian, *The Subterranean Railway: How the London Underground was Built and How it Changed the City Forever* (London: Atlantic Books, 2005, Kindle edition).

Espionage – Trainspotting with a Purpose

Debruyne, Emmanuel, 'Intelligence in Occupied Belgium: The Business of Anglo-Belgian Espionage and Intelligence Cooperation During the Two World Wars (1914–1918, 1940–1944)', in *Intelligence and National Security*, Vol. 28, no. 3, p. 330 (2013).

Dowling, Timothy (ed.), *Personal Perspectives: World War One* (California: ABC CLIO, 2005).

Morgan, Janet, *The Secrets of Rue St Roch* (London: Penguin, 2005).

Morton, James, *Spies of the First World War: Under Cover for King and*

Kaiser (Kew: National Archives, 2010).

Occleshaw, Michael, *Armour Against Fate: Military Intelligence in the Twentieth Century* (London: Columbus, 1988).

http://www.bl.uk/world-war-one/articles/civilian-atrocities-german-1914

Supplying the Fleet

Tucker, Spencer C. (ed.), *The Encyclopedia of World War I: A Political, Social, and Military History* (Santa-Barbara: ABC-CLIO, 2005).

http://www.bl.uk/world-war-one/articles/the-war-at-sea

The Armistice Carriage

Lowry, Bullitt, *Armistice 1918* (Ohio: Kent State University Press, 1996).

Tucker, Spencer C., *The European Powers in the First World War: An Encyclopedia* (Oxon: Routledge, 2013).

CHAPTER 5 – RAILWAYS AND REMEMBRANCE

Remembering Railwaymen – A Service at St Paul's

Higgins, Jeremy *Great War Railwaymen: Britain's Railway Company Workers at War 1914–1918* (Brighton: Firestep Publishing, 2014).

Massie, Robert K., *Castles of Steel. Britain, Germany and the Winning of the Great War at Sea* (London: Jonathan Cape, 2004).

Railway Gazette: Special War Transportation Number (Stockport: The Moseley Railway Trust, 2013 [first edition by the *Railway Gazette*, 1920]).

http://www.1914.org/podcasts/podcast-18-mesopotamia/

A Railway Martyr Returns

Allen, Cecil J., *The Great Eastern Railway* (London: Ian Allan Ltd., 1975).

Bridgeland, Tony, *Outrage at Sea: Naval Atrocities of the First World War* (Barnsley: Leo Cooper, 2002).

Janes, Brian, *The Unknown Warrior and the Cavell Van* (Tenterden: Kent & East Sussex Railway, 2010).

Railway Pilgrims to the Western Front – Battlefield Tourism is Born

British Legion, in cooperation with the British Empire Service League, *Battlefields Pilgrimage 1928* (London, 1928). Available online at http://www.mkheritage.co.uk/wfa/photo_galleries/BL_pilgrimage_gallery/index.html

British Legion, *A Souvenir of the Battlefields Pilgrimage (August, 1928)* (London: Press Printers, 1929).

Lloyd, David W., *Battlefield Tourism: Pilgrimage and the Commemoration of the Great War in Britain, Australia and Canada, 1919–1939* (Oxford: Berg, 1998).

Britain's Railways After the Armistice – The Beginning of the End of the Line?

Bonavia, Michael R., *The Four Great Railways* (Newton Abbott: David & Charles, 1980).

Vaughan, Adrian, *Railwaymen, Politics and Money: The Great Age of Railways in Britain* (London: John Murray, 1997).

INDEX

Italic page references
indicate illustrations